The Zen Factor
Tools for Success

Jacqueline Hope

eQuil Books

eQuil Books

Published by eQuil Books

PO Box 511, Main Beach, Queensland 4217, Australia

equilbooks@fastmail.fm

All rights reserved.

Copyright © 2013 by Jacqueline Hope

The moral right of the author has been asserted. No part of this book may be reproduced by any means, other than as brief quotations in other works or reviews without written permission of the publisher.

National Library of Australia

Cataloguing-in-Publication data

Hope, Jacqueline

The zen factor : tools for success / Jacqueline Hope.

1. Small business. 2. Self-actualization (Psychology).

3. Spiritual formation. 4. Strategic planning.

I. Title.

Dewey Number: 338.642

ISBN: 978-0-9874711-1-6 (Print version)

Cover photo: Sunset at Huon Reef

"When you throw a stone into the water, it hurries by the swiftest possible path to the bottom. It is like this when Siddhartha has a goal, a resolve. His goal draws him to it, for he allows nothing into his soul that might conflict with this goal. It is what fools call magic and think it is performed by demons. Anyone can perform magic. Anyone can reach his goals." - Hermann Hesse, Siddhartha.

For my children and theirs.
Standing on the shoulders of our forebears,
they begin where I leave off.

CONTENTS

Introduction 1

SECTION I:

CLEARING THE PATH 7

Chapter 1: Financial freedom 9

Chapter 2: The leap of faith 24

Chapter 3: Knowing what works 39

Chapter 4: Out on the skinny branches 54

Chapter 5: Removing the blocks 79

Chapter 6: Practising success 98

Chapter 7: Beyond limits 111

SECTION II:

BUILDING YOUR DREAMS 129

Chapter 8: Expansion 131

Chapter 9: The shape of dreams 146

Chapter 10: Keeping on track 160

Chapter 11: Interpretations 178

Chapter 12: Other influences 192

SECTION III:

THE WAY THINGS CAN BE 207

Chapter 13: The problem or the answer 209

Chapter 14: The trail to now 223

Chapter 15: Redefining success 238

Chapter 16: Acts of creation 249

Chapter 17: Accepting change 262

About the author 277

Introduction

Zen: a unified state of being that involves dropping illusions and seeing things without distortion or judgment.

Whilst the main focus of *"The Zen Factor"* is on finding success through the development of your own business, it is also about finding balance, peace, harmony and happiness in the whole of your life. What would success be without these? One of the preconditions for the realization of your deepest desires is mastery of self, which is a corollary of freedom. So this is also a book about finding freedom, on all levels. To my mind, success and freedom are inseparable, but I don't use the word in the ordinary sense. It will be explored in depth throughout this book, and hopefully the meanings behind the symbols will become a self-sustaining part of you through the application of the practical tools offered here.

Freedom is an overused word, seldom understood. To put a different spin on Rousseau's famous quote: "man is born free and everywhere is in chains", we can understand that it is our inner freedom, rather than our outer, that is more often lacking. When asked the question, what is freedom? many think in terms of its opposite, i.e. of not being physically restricted or of not being able to do exactly as one pleases within the confines of society. The absence of freedom is nowhere more evident than in the chains that bind us from within.

Some of the outward signs of a lack of inner freedom are anger, frustration, temper-tantrums or uncontrolled outbursts and petulant sulking. These can stem from a lack of patience, taking oneself too seriously and the inability to buoyantly rise above adversity whilst maintaining one's equanimity. This impatience robs us of learning opportunities and keeps us bound to our undeveloped selves. You might even think we are describing a two year-old here and indeed most of our inner bondage is a direct result of our not growing up.

The same lack of freedom is present when we have no control over our thoughts, not realizing the power they have over us and the world we experience. (This is where we carry the two year-old along with us into adulthood). Uncontrolled thoughts are constantly playing out their dramas in our minds, pushing and pulling us in various directions, creating worlds of worries. A whole string of negative thoughts are known as worries, and these can cause us huge problems, from sleeplessness to breakdown. Our worries seem to have a life of their own quite beyond our control. We all too readily relinquish responsibility for them, and again, freedom is lost. It is this inner freedom that is the measure of a successful life.

There are a number of different aspects to

success, including financial, physical, mental, emotional and spiritual. For each of these, the same principles apply and there are a great many resources, tools and strategies available for achieving success on all levels. This book contains a collection of my personal favorites as well as several of my own making. I can attest to their power in delivering results. It was through their use that I was able to find my own way out of bondage.

Even though the primary focus of *"The Zen Factor"* is financial freedom you will soon see that the quickest way to achieve this is by first seeking inner freedom. Zen is the experiential awareness of truth that sets you free. In reality, we already *are* truth, but we have forgotten that, just as we already are free, but have forgotten that too. There are a great many things we have forgotten and it is this that causes so much suffering in our lives. A person lacking freedom has a very limited, often unhappy existence. Happiness and freedom go hand in hand. In order to find the way out of our cages we need a guide, which is what this book is. It is something of a treasure map, but it cannot do the digging for you. It is not a quick fix or substitute for your own effort. But it can show you where and how it pays to apply that effort. It makes sense to utilize available tools as a shortcut.

In subsequent chapters you will find a great many tools for success. Through applying them to my own small business development, I was able to make over a million dollars in less than three years. Many outside observers of this phenomenon have asked me how, in the hope that the strategies I used are replicable. I believe them to be so.

There is an old saying that goes: "first tether your camel". What this means is that unless the basic needs such as food and shelter are taken care of, there is little chance of seeking anything more. Prior to nourishing the spirit the body must first be nourished. It is a largely inescapable fact that we all need money to live. Those of us who are in paid employment have traded their time for money. This could be seen as a kind of modern-day slavery, sometimes expressed as having "sold one's soul". We are bound by a contract that says we will attend to whatever duties we must, in order to receive our pay.

While some of us are fortunate enough to enjoy their daily occupation, many find it a burden and an undesirable necessity. Longevity in a repetitive role can indeed be soul-destroying. And no matter how long a paid position lasts, there is always the fear of losing it, which creates a constant, underlying insecurity. If your job security depends upon your employer's good or bad fortunes, you can never be sure of your future income, or indeed your very survival in a cash-based society. If the company is struggling, workers get laid off. We can see this happening at the moment on a global scale.

One way to escape this uncertainty is to run your own business. Of course it would be naive to think of a fledgling business as being immune to external economic forces, but there are ways of building success even in uncertain times. As already mentioned, mastery of self leads to mastery of results. Without having the self-discipline to push against adversity, we cannot develop strong ventures. We need to learn how to avoid the common pitfalls, how to create healthy, sustainable enterprises, and most of all, how to be the driver of our own carriage.

It is important to find new ways of being that are courageous; we must be willing to explore different approaches and to take full responsibility for outcomes. We cannot pass the buck. If we wish to live in a better place, it is to be of our own making and we need to know this. It takes self-awareness and self-control. There are specific tools for achieving these qualities which are contained in this book. It is up to you to apply them and you will be amply rewarded for doing so.

SECTION I

CLEARING THE PATH

Chapter 1

Financial freedom

Two questions have been asked of me: "how did I make more than a million dollars in less than three years?" And secondly, "how could I walk away from it all at the end of that time?" I am never sure which of these two has been the more intriguing to observers. This book is an attempt to answer these questions and hopefully to inspire others to also follow their dreams. A very battered, well-used copy of *"A Course In Miracles"* has provided much of my inspiration and I often consider one of its profound questions: "Do I want the problem or do I want the answer?" And most reassuringly the response: "Decide for the answer and you will have it, for you will see it as it is, and it is yours already." Before we can begin to understand the full significance of this statement we must first clear the path.

I came across an interesting reference recently that stated that of the 30 billion individual species believed to have ever existed on earth, only a hundredth of one percent survives today. Clearly survival depends on adaptability. So far we have demonstrated sufficient ability in this regard to have allowed the continuing evolution and existence of humankind. Change is the one constant that cannot be ignored. This is evident in every aspect of our lives and particularly noticeable in that sector which consumes the majority of our waking hours: our occupation. If you have ever considered taking control of this side of your life you are in good company. This is the path that many have found is the one most likely to lead toward financial freedom. This is where challenges precipitate change most readily.

A new model for corporate success is emerging in the 21st century. Businesses that cling to the old ways of manipulation, force and hierarchical control through fear will be the dinosaurs of the future. The reign they have enjoyed has come at too costly a price, both to individuals and to the planet. It is unsustainable. Their traditional structures are shaped like triangles instead of circles, with the few elite bosses at the pinnacle controlling the assumed mindless masses at the base. Instead of pulling together, people stand in opposition to one another. These divisive elements of opposition generate profits at the expense of people through exploitation and greed. There is no upward communication, other than complaint. There is no mutuality, empathy, trust or co-operation. Other aspects of life, such as pleasure, family and friends are often subordinated to work and there is a singular sense of being 'driven', rather than being the driver. Is this an image of success? Or is there a better way?

It has been written that "leadership is the process of fully becoming oneself." (Warren Bennis, "*On Becoming A Leader*"). This puts a different perspective on the conventional view of leadership, linking it instead to the notion that mastery of self precedes mastery of others. Self knowledge, self awareness and self control are part of the process of fully becoming oneself and form an integral part of the creation of a successful business. There can be no doubt that there is a creative force in starting up a new business. Creation is a holistic, multi-faceted force that includes all aspects of life as well as a connection to the whole.

In a holistically operated, successful business, there is the creation of innovative ideas, services or high quality products. There is a sense of purpose, integrity and contribution through relationships which are mutually supportive, with the utmost respect always being shown. There is an ethos of exceptional service, above and beyond expectations, to clients, employees, communities, stakeholders and self. An atmosphere of consideration, trust and co-operation is created, with provision for life's demands as well as for fun. There is open communication with colleagues, employees, clients and investors. It is not a one-sided endeavor with a bottom-line of profit above all else. There is no dichotomy of work versus life;

money versus time, as is seen in the triangular model of opposition and competition.

When we are fully in relation with others, we grow in all respects. We are able to integrate personal meaning along with the attainment of financial success. The new business paradigm integrates profits with meaning, upholding respect for ourselves, for others and for our environment. What was once considered idealistic or fringe, will come to be recognized as vital to our survival.

Finding balance

Success may be measured comparatively, against the achievements of others, or as a personal best, against one's own. The former criteria can never be complete. No matter how many hurdles you jump, the bar can always be raised. The latter is much more dependable. Setting benchmarks and goals that are achievable within our own timeframe is something we all can do. But it is important to maintain a balance in our endeavors and to take responsibility for our actions.

There are many different aspects involved in a holistic view of success: personal, social, financial, spiritual, etc. To focus on one to the detriment of another creates a state of imbalance. Eventually this creates tension, a pull one way or another, that precedes a toppling. A simple pie-graph provides a reminder for us to check the balance:

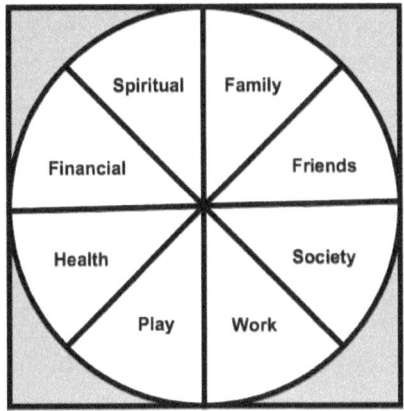

The sectors shown here (family, friends, society, work, play, health, financial and spiritual) are neither definitive nor exhaustive – they can be added to or subtracted according to individual need. Of course there are limitations with such a schematic representation. Life cannot be so neatly compartmentalized and it would be naive to think that we can pay equal attention to each facet. The key concept here is not to focus overly much on one part of our lives to the detriment of another, as for example in sacrificing quality time with our families for the sake of making more money, or spending hours each day in meditation instead of paying attention to our body's need for physical exercise.

The pie-graph is simplistic but still useful. Each of us will have a different interpretation of what each of the sectors stands for in our lives. But whichever way we look at it, we can easily identify those areas that are important to us and those that are being neglected. It is not hard to spot the deficits, because they are like a buckled bicycle wheel, creaking and squeaking in ways that will eventually grind everything to a halt. If millions of dollars are pouring in each year, but family, friends, or personal health are suffering, how rewarding is that?

A lack of balance is not good for businesses or for people. Long days in the office and work brought home after hours, no time off, no down-time, no fun, used to be the image of the serious, ambitious businessperson. But along with that image went varying degrees of stress, discontent and depression. A brief survey of the surrounding landscape revealed further unrest, with families in disarray and the breakdown of social support structures. Add to these the anxiety of global financial crises, uncertainty about the competency of our leaders, as well as of the future of our planet. We live in times of rapid change and part of that change is taking place in the way we run our businesses.

Exploring new possibilities

It is not surprising to learn that these days, some of the more successful companies are places where qualities like passion, enthusiasm and lateral thinking are encouraged and the daily grind is replaced with a more adventurous 'sand-box' approach, where workers can be like young children who are free to have fun, explore and be themselves. Such a workplace environment encourages people to be wholly present, rather than bringing to work only the parts that are directly useful to the company. Each of us has talents and ideas to offer that may otherwise be overlooked.

When the whole person is present, there will be creativity and laughter. There will be playfulness, a willingness to take risks and step out on the skinny branches. Contributions that are unexpected or surprising are highly valued and respected. Edward de Bono, author of *"Serious Fun"* and *"Lateral Thinking"* has written: "You set out to move things about and to build them up, and even though you don't quite know what you are going to do, something suggests itself out of what you have already got. Far too many adults lack the ability to play around and "see what happens.""

There is a sense of exploration and adventure which is inherent to all of our true natures. When we are free of fears - fear of looking foolish, fear of ridicule, fear of failure - we are free to move more boldly into the unknown. This spirit is nurtured in our early childhood and then forgotten in later life, when we get down to the more serious business of living. Then the spirit of adventure is seen as inappropriate or even dangerous, and whimsical musing is considered a waste of time. But it has been well recognized that productivity increases in a more light-hearted environment, tasks are accomplished more efficiently and fewer sick days are taken. The courageous entrepreneur can create such an environment and all will reap the benefits.

Your wildest dreams

When the focus is shifted from the ends to the means, the journey itself provides the rewards and financial growth provides the means. Fewer business owners these days are only in it for the money. Some have combined this goal with the higher purpose of doing good in the world, effecting positive change while avoiding harming others or the environment. This is not to say they ignore the numerical bottom line but they are more aware of their operations' impact and have a more responsible attitude to the consequences. For them, financial growth enables growth of self, contribution to others, to community and to the planet.

By paying attention to the various sectors of the above pie-graph, regularly checking in on how each is faring, we can merge personal growth along with fiscal growth. Fortunately, there are many tools at our disposal to assist us in becoming more attuned to what's important in life and for remembering the things we have forgotten. Some of these strategies will seem rather ordinary, simply echoing what we already know, though even these provide a useful reminder for when we are distracted. Others will seem outlandish and beyond belief, requiring us to withhold skepticism and what we think we already know.

I ask you to allow yourself to open up to a different perspective, another possibility. It's always helpful to have another possibility available, when the old ones are letting us down. Sometimes it is necessary to step right out of what we know, of what we are comfortable with, and allow something wild and wonderful in. Our wildest dreams need not remain just that. It is possible to turn them into reality, as I discovered.

Remembering

With no prior business experience I drew instead on other, less commonly used resources that I already had within me. These form the practical means of accessing what I refer to as the Zen Factor and are quite replicable by others who take the time to learn them. Even though any attempt at definition is limiting, one way to think of Zen is as a total state of focus that incorporates a unity of body, mind and spirit.

It seems odd that a word as Asian as 'Zen' should

have an Indo-European origin, but it has in fact been in the English language since 1727. A more recent understanding sees Zen as part of a school of Mahayana Buddhism that asserts that enlightenment can be attained through meditation, self-contemplation, and intuition. Zen is a way of being present to the present. It involves dropping illusions and seeing things without distortion or judgment. Above all, it is a practical method of attaining freedom through personal awakening. Another term for awakening is remembering. This removes any sense of struggle to attain something that is not already present, right here and now.

This is not a text of theoretical conjecture or wild forays into the unknown. It is firmly grounded in the physical world, despite presenting some ideas that may seem quite contrary to the norm. (If it didn't, we would be left with only that - the norm!) It contains a great many practical methods for achieving personal transformation and the realization of your heart's desire.

My early dreams

My own dream was an ocean-going yacht and the time to sail it. I wanted to "buy the rest of my life", without taking the rest of my life to do so. It seems I was born with salt-water in my veins, as they say of those of us in love with the sea, though no-one else in my family seemed to have the same affliction. My father's family hailed from Yorkshire, which is where I was born. My mother was Greek, so that could account for some seafaring ancestry, though having been a child bride, she left us when my brother was four and I was two years old.

It couldn't have been easy for my father to raise two young children alone, but he did make some good decisions. One was to emigrate to the warmer climes of New Zealand; the other was to buy an old timber cottage perched on the edge of a cliff with a magnificent view over a protected estuary. So I had the good fortune of growing up in a small beachside community with little parental supervision. Child protection agencies put paid to that freedom and a long string of single-parent housekeepers came along with their own offspring and tried to rule the roost. Most were cruel to their own children and to us so didn't last long.

When I was about seven years old, my favorite arrived, a half-cast Maori woman, whose two brothers were boat-builders living not far down the road from us. Visiting their vast timber boat sheds was an experience beyond rapture for me and I longed to know the thrill of being afloat. Each of the brothers built their sons a magnificent, fully varnished P-class yacht and I watched the process in awe. They waxed and polished the hulls to a mirror-finish and sat them on carpeted cradles on the beach amongst the other less perfect examples of the class. The two boys won every race they entered whilst I looked on longingly.

Being a typical Yorkshire man, with the recognized condition of short arms and deep pockets, our father bought a very leaky, knocked-about sailing dinghy and said to my brother and me, "whichever one of you learns to sail it first can have it." Even though I knew nothing about sailing, I was as tantalized as a teased kitten and could scarcely control my excitement.

"It's mine," I said, whereupon my older brother most disinterestedly replied, "You can have it".

And so began a life-long love affair with the sea. Virtually every day I would be dragging that little boat down the sand to the water, rigging her up and teaching myself how to sail. Every Saturday afternoon I paid my entry fee and honed my skills in racing. Over the years, I bought and sold at least another dozen small boats, always doing them up for resale at a slight profit, obviously business-minded even then. And always dreaming of sailing across oceans, sometime in the future, when I had a big enough yacht and the time to do it. So in many ways my future dreams came into this world with me, as can be seen in many a youngster, with a passion for doing whatever it is they love most.

Finding purpose

One of the most commonly asked questions is how to find our own calling or life's purpose. Perhaps the most obvious way is through this burning desire that seems to have been a part of us for as long as we can remember. If you don't have any awareness of such passion, it can be developed through the use of the tools in this book. Let your heart be your guide to what inspires you and draws you. Find those involvements which have meaning to you personally, then turn them into your own creation. By creating and following your own dreams, you discover your purpose.

If life hasn't yet moved you to begin your own business, look around you and notice what is needed. Successful entrepreneurs recognize needs and fill them. There are literally thousands of possible ventures waiting to be recognized and the one that grabs your attention is likely to be the one that resonates with your own interests or talents. Whatever you eventually settle on as an interesting pursuit need not be something you or others believe you are already good at, nor even something that will necessarily guarantee you great wealth; it can come from left field but always contains a knowing that this is right for you. It speaks to you softly like a lover's whisper.

For me, the sea spoke to me in the thousands

of hours I spent with it whilst growing up. The peace and solitude encouraged practice in a deep listening and provided the answers to many a perplexing question I brought with me from the land. It was my best friend, my family, my mentor and teacher. So it was natural that this would provide the impetus I needed when the time came, much later in life, to find the means that would allow my lifelong dreams to become reality.

But as is more often the case in the modern business paradigm, it wasn't only about me. I also wanted to contribute to society in a meaningful way and create something of benefit to others. I wanted to be part of the answer, rather than the problem; to be a cause rather than an effect. By then, I knew that giving is receiving and that mastery of self precedes mastery of results. The sea provided me with many lessons in all these things and led me to devote my life to their further exploration through various studies and practices. I pass some of these on to you here.

My suggestion is to treat this text as a kind of work-book, extracting from it what is useful and leaving the rest. It may help to transcribe relevant sections to create one's own 'recipe book' for success, adding to it as it evolves beyond this starting point. Remember though, a recipe is not the meal! It requires a hands-on effort of application to translate it into something that will sustain us. And every cook will produce a different outcome from the same ingredients. This adds spice to life.

Throughout the journey, I utilized the specific tools described in this book to help keep me on track. I didn't always succeed. The ideal situation is to live more fully in the present, to practice equanimity, love and compassion. These are the pre-conditions for finding the inner peace and happiness that we all seek. I have often fallen short. There were many instances when 'the wheels fell off' or I simply forgot what was most important. There were times when I doubted everything and felt like quitting. But then if the path did not have its obstacles, would it be so rewarding? Perfection is an ideal that few of us attain – but all of us can benefit from its guiding light.

Chapter 2

The leap of faith

Starting up your own business is a leap into the unknown that is both challenging and exhilarating. One thing is certain, you will be stretched beyond your comfort zone - especially if this is as unfamiliar territory to you as it was to me. As a novice small business owner, you will need to develop a repertoire of new skills, from bookkeeping to marketing. Or you may already know these things, which will certainly give you a head start. A practical nature will help, although this can also be a limiting factor, preventing you from stretching into unfamiliar, playful or even bizarre territory.

My own natural tendency is to be quite practical and logical minded, looking for rational explanations for everything. Experience has opened me up to deeper contemplations, allowing at least for the existence of the inexplicable. If you cannot remain open to the mysteries of life, you will miss out on a great deal. Like the dinosaurs, you will become unsuited to your environment, and your environment will likewise reject you. A heaviness and tedium will wear you down; each step will be slow and forced. Calcification of both mind and body will follow.

Thankfully there is another realm in which we can play, one in which a higher energy lifts us up to our true station in life. The more ineffable, lighter realms challenge us to broaden our horizons, open us to unexpected synchronicities and round us out to become more complete human beings. This is where we dip our toes in deep waters, rekindle our playful side and sway more freely in the breeze. This is where we extend the inner child into a natural maturity that combines a deep connection with the way things are, with the power to create our lives in accordance with our desires.

As already mentioned, my desire was an ocean-going yacht and the time to sail it. It grew from a pasttime that fostered adventure and risk-taking, leading to a life with more emphasis on freedom and personal growth than on the security of working for others. Starting up my own small business seemed to satisfy those needs to some extent. The challenges that are an important part of our self development were there. The autonomy was there and the connection between effort and reward. The potential was there. It held my interest and drew out unrecognized skills. It was deeply satisfying in itself.

What I was completely unprepared for was the rapidity of the realization of my dreams. I knew I wanted to buy the rest of my life without taking the rest of my life to do so, but certainly never expected that to occur in less than three years from start-up. This made me (and others around me) question what was going on. It had to be something different from the norm. This book is an attempt to explain it and to share some of the tools I used along the way. It is not relevant to go into any great description of my own business here, other than to share some pertinent examples of situations that might be commonly encountered.

The driver

There are many different kinds of possible businesses, but basically all offer products and/or services, which are mass producible. So what kind of business to start? You might have absolutely no idea and begin by searching out an unfilled need. You might inherit a family business and develop it into your own. Some will choose to base their business on their present field of expertise - be it jewelry-making, carpentry or sewing clothes. If that is the case, it is important to retain the passion of the craftsman, the inner you who is in love with what you do, who strives to always do it to the best of your ability. This is the heart of the business.

To this will later be added the uncomplaining stoicism of the floor sweeper, the book-keeper, the toilet-cleaner and the dish-washer. The so-called glamorous roles and the more mundane tasks carry equal weight and must be approached with equal devotion to detail (if not passion). Such equality of purpose and acceptance of all things without judgment is part of not taking ourselves too seriously. Parenting provided me with a good background for many of these, training in patience and steadfastness. All tasks can be done with care and attention.

Everyone will have their personal strengths in areas they feel best suited to and it makes sense to build on existing skills. Certain abilities come more naturally to some than to others. Most career paths promote specialization for the sake of efficiency. If you were working as a small cog in a big wheel you would have the luxury of focusing on that one area of expertise. This is not the case in a small business, run initially by only one or two people. Starting out alone means learning how to handle whatever needs to be done. However, that is what makes it all so interesting. You are not just one small cog; you are the whole wheel.

An enormous sense of satisfaction comes from seeing something through from beginning to end. For work to be satisfying it must have these three qualities: interest, autonomy and an obvious connection between effort and reward. The process is the important thing, and brings a deep understanding of choices and consequences. If I am intensely interested in the process,

I am more likely to give it my best shot. When I see the results of my actions, I gain valuable feedback to adjust the process. When I am operating from a place of integrity and wholeness, I can be confident that the process will flow smoothly. When one learns how to be the driver instead of the passenger, the next step is to choose the road. Then it doesn't matter how challenging or difficult it is. Most of all, it is the more testing aspects that provide an opportunity for personal growth. All of life is a lesson in self-knowledge and the more knowledge we have of ourselves, the more we are able to deal with anything. Remember, mastery of self precedes mastery of results.

The direction

Every day thousands of proud creators of small businesses start off, full of high hopes, only to collapse before they cash their first check. There are many excellent books available, explaining in great detail what I call the 'nuts and bolts' of how to run your business successfully. These provide important foundation stones to build upon and can help bridge the gap where knowledge is lacking. In their pages, you will be reassured to know you can convert your existing skills, for example from domestic budgeting into company bookkeeping. And for the most part, anyone with basic intelligence can learn these things. But there is more to success than this.

Operating a small business provides the perfect platform for growth in all respects. It opens up possibilities and opportunities. It brings the satisfaction of creating something that is a personal reflection of ourselves and beyond. In this regard, it almost is like giving birth. It is the creation of something new, where there was nothing before; something that no-one else could create in quite the same way. Some will put their own name to it, like Henry Ford, Yves Saint-Laurent, Levi Straus or Gabrielle (Coco) Chanel. Many will begin with scarcely any idea of what they are letting themselves in for. They often know what they don't want, more than what they do want. They know they don't want to be stuck in the soul-destroying daily grind of mindless activity. They don't want to suffer the indignity of being treated like an imbecile by their 'superiors'. They don't want that loss of connection with end results that comes from being a small cog in a big wheel. They may know they do want to be their own boss, to call the shots, to have the naming rights, to see something through from beginning to end, to have the final say in how things should develop and when the timing is right for new growth spurts, when their baby is ready to walk or run.

Being in business is basically a decision-making process, from start to finish. Every day important decisions must be made, often on the spur of the moment: "This colored packaging or that one? This size ad or that? This promotional campaign or not? This month or next? This employee or that one?" And just as depression stems from a sense of powerlessness, so the converse is true. Huge satisfaction comes from feeling one is master of one's own life. Whether the decisions are wise or hasty, well-founded or haphazard, they are at least one's own. No-one else is telling you what to do. It is your show. Whichever type of show you choose to run, you can be sure it will be challenging, exciting, and rewarding. It will provide opportunities for growth on every level. The rewards that come from being the driver and choosing the direction are endless.

The motivation

But that is only part of the reason to start up a business. Of course, there is also the pecuniary interest - the "what's in it for me?" This is where the connection between effort and reward becomes tangible. Success is often measured in this way, with reference to cash flow as concrete proof that what we are offering has value to others. If our goods or services are attractive enough, useful enough, necessary enough then it follows that people will be willing to pay for them. This in itself provides us with feedback to either continue with more of the same or to make some modifications until we achieve the positive reinforcement that we originally expected. It would be foolish for those expectations not to be spelled out in advance. They form part of the aims we set ourselves from the beginning. We need to know where we are headed and also why.

Some people are motivated by money for its own sake, enjoying watching its accumulation and believing that having a seven figure bank balance somehow confers social status and importance. Even these Scrooges will open up the coffers from time to time with ostentatious public displays of their worth. Others, like myself, start out with some kind of dream of what that money can buy, such as a waterfront mansion, or an ocean going yacht. In many ways, having an actual thing in mind, with an approximate monetary value makes it easier to set the course and to know when we have arrived. It is a tangible object of aspiration.

Some entrepreneurs will have more philanthropic ideals, seeking to assist others less fortunate than themselves with direct financial aid. Sometimes the enormous satisfaction of providing charitable works is something that follows on from having achieved sufficient wealth and already owning more than enough tangible objects of desire. Having enough to be able to give some away is a privileged position to be in and another observable measure of success on the material level.

Others might aim to assist through the provision of beneficial products or services, whilst simultaneously avoiding harm. Whichever path one takes, all have the opportunity to provide dignity through inclusion and interconnectedness, to help restore the balance, to give back what has been taken. It is possible to adopt a head, heart and hands approach, to appreciate the contribution of even the smallest player, to help develop unrecognized strengths and talents. If a business can incorporate these ideals, it is bound to flourish and its richness will be expressed on all levels.

The end at the beginning

It is a good idea right from the outset to ask yourself some salient questions about exactly what it is you want from your endeavors. What is the aim of the game? Is it to help others, and if so, how? Is it to grow personally through the expression of your true self? Is it to build an empire bigger than McDonalds? Is it to spend more time with family or to contribute to the community in some meaningful way? Or to build an island resort or to buy a place on the next space shuttle to Mars? Where are you headed?

As already mentioned, my own simple dream was an ocean-going yacht and the time to sail it. I soon discovered that time is one of the hardest things of all to buy. It is relatively easy to buy material objects, but time, especially if that embraces a comfortable lifestyle, is not so easy. Wanting to buy the rest of my life presented quite a challenge. Retirement is not such an uncommon goal but it's wise to think it through clearly in advance, in every nuance, as much as is possible. Remember the old saying, "be careful what you ask for, because you just might get it."

It's not so easy to see clearly into a future that has yet to develop and we can fool ourselves into imagining utopian scenarios that we have extrapolated from cameo scenes. A brief interlude of time out from our regular daily activities can provide a kind of sampler to help identify what alternative things we enjoy doing. Sometimes, the intensity of a short holiday away can be exhausting, as we try to cram into a couple of weeks all the fun we have missed out on during the year and we return from our break feeling as though we need a holiday. It would be unrealistic to imagine that such a frenetic pace could be sustained indefinitely. Even the most delicious food can become sickly if that becomes what we must eat every day, for the rest of our lives.

Quite a few people dream of an early retirement

but then have nothing to fill their empty days with. They miss the days of active employment and the social status that confers. They miss the sense of self-importance and power. If they try to wield that power outside of the corporate world they soon discover it is not well received by their peers. They can easily become like 'grumpy old men', grumbling discontentedly about everything that is not to their liking. They find themselves shifting downward in the pecking order of the barnyard, from loudly crowing cockerels to sickly old roosters. It is not an uncommon scenario for death to be waiting in the side-wings within a year of retirement. Many retirees have no sense of community apart from with former work colleagues and have no way of finding this lost connection once they are out on their own. It is yet another result of having led an unbalanced life, with excessive focus on career path, financial gain or unbridled ambition.

What color is the back door?

Western society has done a good job in firmly establishing the strong Protestant work ethic. Our careers are how we define ourselves and once that is removed, our sense of self can flounder. We all have to be something in order to justify our existence. We are defined by our roles and habitually answer the question, "what do you do?" with an "I am a ……" answer. "I am an accountant." Or

"I am a teacher." Ok, that sums you up; now we know where you fit, or more importantly *that* you fit. It is often these inner things, far more than economic need that keep people from drawing a line in the sand and choosing when they will let go of paid employment. Although of course there are also those who have no understanding of how much is enough and feel compelled to keep on making more, with no real thought of what for. And then there are those who are caught up in the ride and don't know how to find the stop button. They have never paid any attention to the back door.

This relates to the questions asked of me that I mentioned in the beginning of this book: "how did I make more than a million dollars in less than three years?" and: "how could I walk away from it all at the end of that time?" The answer to how and when to exit gracefully is always a personal decision and it pays to explore the questions and answers around this topic as honestly as possible. Don't leave this major decision ignored or chances are the back door will blur into a cleverly camouflaged wall. You need to know how to deal with these things in advance. How to be able to predetermine the finish line? What do I want and when do I want it by? These are important issues that need to be addressed, and quite early on in the game. Again, it is part of the process of fully becoming oneself, of knowing one's strengths and weaknesses, one's true nature. It is sometimes beneficial to enlist outside help in this process, to help find answers to the hard questions, such as "how comfortable do I feel without my career label to define me?"; "How would I spend my days?"

And then what?

One consideration lies in the difference between paid employment and unpaid engagement in some other interesting activity. Whilst the latter might include sport or hobbies or some kind of volunteer work, few would find the same sense of satisfaction in rolling these over into full-time occupations. It has been noted that personal happiness is increased through a sense of meaningful contribution to society. In other words, not many are prepared to adopt a 'drop-out' mentality. It is not unusual to find retired executives starting up some small hobby business in their spare time. It is not that they need the money; it is often all that they know how to do. The multi-millionaire next door to my father's, for example, now in his 80's is still carving up land and developing commercial properties, even though it often raises public antagonism and causes him a great deal of stress that he doesn't need. Why does he do it? "What else would I do?" he asks.

So it is worthwhile developing a game-plan that

includes the back door and more importantly, knowing what is on the other side of that door. Not everyone wants to sail around the world. Some would prefer to fly to exotic locations to lie on the beach sipping margaritas. Some would simply like more time to spend with family and friends, having the luxury and ease of a no-rush lifestyle, taking the time to stop and smell the roses.

There is a wonderful story of a highly-stressed executive who gets to escape the daily grind for a hard-earned vacation to a beautiful tropical island paradise. There, he encounters one of the local people sitting on a log, tossing pebbles into the crystal clear water, watching the ring of ripples echo and fade. They talk about their different lifestyles, the executive relating the importance of his work. He explains his ambitions and future projections and all the steps he must climb to reach the top of the ladder.

"And then what?" asks the local.

The executive smiles, "Then I will have enough money to be able to sit somewhere like this and throw pebbles in the water."

We might chuckle at the irony of this tale but it illustrates the point quite well. Which of the two men is the richer? Generally we define wealth in terms of money but there are so many other aspects to it that cannot be weighed or measured. Take just one, for example, health. What do we have if our health has been sacrificed by stress?

The old-school business paradigm was a hard one within which to find a balance between work and all other aspects of life. In the old corporate world, people became brittle and broken and this was the accepted and even expected way things were. Fortunately there is a new way, which is much gentler, more humane, more creative – and ultimately, more successful on all levels. It is becoming easier to recognize the outdated dinosaurs and their impact on the world. It is heavy-handed, damaging and unsustainable. The new business paradigm has the advantage of using this stepping stone to leap from. Recognizing the mistakes of the past enables us to move ahead into unchartered waters with a confidence built on the wealth of information now available to us.

Chapter 3

Knowing what works

Now it is time to answer the first of the two questions asked of me: "How did I make a million in less than three years?" This is the exciting part of the journey, the part which will challenge your preconceptions and ask for a willing suspension of disbelief. Begin with an open mind and be prepared to explore some different ideas, new ways of looking at old ideas and for a shift from horizontal to vertical perception. It is not necessary to understand everything intellectually for it to be effective. Indeed, there are many things that fall into that category. *"A Course in Miracles"* tells us that it is only necessary to follow the curriculum, to consistently meditate on its 365 daily lessons in order to integrate the truth of its teachings. Each day is an opportunity to learn and to grow. Using the tools presented in this book will bring conviction in the ability, because conviction comes through accomplishment.

A concept known as 'synergy' encompasses the idea that the whole is much greater than the sum of all its parts. When we gather various bits and pieces together they form another entity which can no longer be defined by reference to its individual parts. This new entity has developed a life of its own which is many times more powerful than logic would predict. There are many other examples of the inexplicable, such as 'time', which can be fun to think about, but the important thing to consider is always usefulness. Is it something you can use in any way? Certainly it helps to have some kind of understanding of how something, for example, electricity, works, but at the end of the day, it is far more valuable to know *that* it works.

There are basically two ways of making your business work: one is by the sheer force of your own personal effort, which will wear you down over time. You may eventually succeed, but it will take a very, very long time and the costs will be huge. This is the way of the dinosaurs, heavy, hard and unsustainable. The other way has sometimes been referred to as "work smarter, not harder". What does that mean? How can we work smarter? How can we be any smarter than we are? The answer is we can't, at least not while operating from our limited, small self that is bound by preconceptions, conditioning and habitual states of unawareness. There exists another way which we can access that is much smarter; indeed, so much so as to be considered guided by omniscience. Imagine having access to that intelligence. Imagine being shown how to access that power. Would you not gladly let go of all you thought you knew? Dr Wayne Dyer in *"The Power of Intention"* wrote: "accessing the power of intention relieved so much of the seemingly impossible work of striving to fulfill my desires by sheer force of will."

Beyond nuts and bolts

If you think of the 'nuts and bolts' of the day-to-day activities of running your business as the physical aspect, there is another, less tangible, some would say 'metaphysical' aspect that is much harder to explain - in fact all attempts to do so always fall short. This has been variously described as input from the unconscious mind, a higher vibrational level, an intuitive sense or a deep knowing. There is a 'rightness' about it, which carries a certainty that what is, could be no other way.

We can all experience this in our daily lives. When we do, we are aware that it is something outside of the norm, that is, it has a paranormal quality to it that is beyond explanation. Nonetheless, there is a recognizable 'flavor' to it; a sense of unity or inter-connectedness of everything and everyone that invariably brings feelings of great awe. For example, couples who have grown together over the years often know what the other is thinking. In a surprising way they might pluck a thought, seemingly out of 'nowhere' that corresponds to something the other was working on or struggling to remember. Despite the years, this still carries an element of surprise and wonderment. "Where did that come from?" or "How did you know I was just about to say that?" or "There's no way known you could have guessed that."

There are many examples in all of our lives of similar phenomena. Elusive information may make itself known to us without us knowing how. How many of us have had the experience of remarkable synchronicities, when exactly the right thing or person turns up at exactly the right time, and we are able to recognize them? It never ceases to amaze us how we manage to find just what we need when it is most needed. We may put this down to mere coincidence, good luck, pure chance or random events that just happen to meet in a fortuitous way, yet on some level we feel intrigued enough to wonder.

Such things are awe-inspiring precisely because we intuitively sense them as in some way coming from outside of ourselves, though most would be reluctant to describe them as involving 'extra-sensory perception' or any other mystical force. It remains an experiential awareness of the inexplicable. We accept this (with awe) as something given, or as something mysterious that can passively just 'happen', but we don't believe it is something we can actively will.

This is a limiting belief that prevents us from experiencing such events as indeed being miracles that we can influence and predict. Their source is the power of mind when aligned with the energy that sustains us all - that beats our heart and breathes our breaths and keeps atoms and molecules doing exactly what they are meant to do in their miraculous perfection. We can choose to be in alignment with this energy and there are specific tools available to show us how, many of which are presented in this book. The synergistic sum of all of their mysterious and ineffable parts is what I am calling the Zen Factor.

The Zen Factor

There is a key factor behind every successful enterprise, whether it is acknowledged or not. To call it the 'Zen Factor' is to refer to the paradoxical contribution of Zen-mind and no-mind; no-thought and all-thought. It is a term that encompasses a vast body of wisdom, derived from an experiential awareness of our true natures and our interconnectedness with all and everything. This is what enables us to step outside of our limited conditioning, to align ourselves with higher energies and to achieve our goals without relying on our own will to push through obstacles. I use the term here as an umbrella concept for the various tools for success presented in this book, recognizing of course that there are many, many more than these and even these are essentially limited, presenting only a thin slice of possibility.

These notions may be quite unfamiliar to some of you but I ask you to put any preconceptions aside for a while and accept the possibility of something else; something that has been described over the millennia by many great thinkers whose works have stood the test of time. While it might be difficult to associate such ideas with the corporate world, I can assure you they are out there, being used to great benefit. It is the utility of an idea that gives it credence.

There are many things that we don't understand yet we make everyday use of, such as the mysterious world of physics or electronics. Most of us use electronic mail (e-mail) on a regular basis, yet few could explain exactly how it works. Stop for a moment to consider the incredible fact that I can type some words on my laptop, which is a finite, self-contained piece of equipment with no visible connection to another. At the push of a button, that message is virtually transferred to anywhere else in the world, where another machine can receive it, decode it and someone else can read it. It is one of those mysteries of life, right up there with wrinkles in time.

Yet, what makes all this so acceptable to us, despite our ignorance of how it works, is the fact that it does (for the most part), reliably work. It is a commonly replicable phenomenon, despite being largely ineffable, except to a few initiated. For the average person, it has a direct causality that can be empirically proven through everyday use, and from this use, a certain meaning ascribed. We can agree that utility precedes meaning. We use it; therefore it has a certain meaning to us. Just like a knife and fork or an airplane.

Meaning

Throughout history meaning has never held constant. Take 'time', for example, once a simple enough linear progression, although even then, with variations on the theme according to which calendar you used. Einstein's theory of relativity gave that a nudge, finding that space also had an effect on things. Time altered according to where you were in space. A clock in a jet plane would be slower than a clock on the ground. Someone standing on earth is moving at about 30 km/sec around the sun, so time observed from the sun will be different again. Einstein's theory of space-time allows for this relativity. The once science fiction concept of 'imaginary time' goes at right angles to regular time, preventing time from curving back on itself, eating its own tail or falling into a black hole. This is a truly mind-boggling thought and there are many others like it.

Take the seemingly bizarre paradigm in quantum mechanics that claims an object has not just a single history but all possible histories and that these can co-exist simultaneously. Science is now able to ratify the reality of the paradox, where an object can both be and not be at the same time. Such concepts open our minds to the prospect of an infinite number of possible realities. This can be either terrifying in its uncertainty, or exciting and liberating, depending on our perspective.

We may usefully consider the Zen Factor as a conduit to the boundlessness of a paradoxical universe, where a unified consciousness supports everything effortlessly and expansion and abundance do not imply a corresponding contraction or loss. The classic example of this paradox is seen in the giving of love, which multiplies as we give it away. Its expansion creates more from more. The wisdom of the ages is contained in this understanding which has been repeated by all the great teachers throughout time, over and over again. There is a potent force available to us that expresses abundance for anyone who taps into it. A greater intelligence guides us along the way, gently reminding us of our perfection. We are on a journey with no beginning, middle or end. We are already here and this is where 'being' precedes 'doing'. "Know first thyself" is an oft repeated maxim.

When we are being true to ourselves, we are

in alignment with our world, our individual sphere of influence, our community, family and friends. Not only this, but far, far beyond. We become a conduit in our own right, through which creative forces far beyond anything we might ordinarily imagine can flow. These are the forces that shape destinies, which open up pathways to our higher good and allow abundance into our lives. The singular, separated individual is as limited as a snail, and relies largely on what he can carry himself. He might be the strongest snail, but his path will be slow and commonplace. There will be no quantum leaps that transform his capabilities into those of an eagle. He is pre-defined and pre-determined.

For those who cling to the way things have always been done, stepping beyond the known is not an option. We can predict their most likely future on the basis of the past. For those who are open to change, who are willing to explore new ideas, anything and everything is possible. There are signposts to follow and tips from those who have paved the way. But all of these would be of little use, without a form to encompass them. That form is very well supplied by running one's own business.

Happenstance

'Happenstance', or the confluence of circumstance, is an interesting thing to consider. There are pivotal moments in all of our lives, when the planets seem to line up, or when we just seem to be in the right place at the right time. We all know of someone who has happened upon the perfect house, or job, car or boat that is exactly right for them. Things like this can even seem to disappear from view, almost becoming invisible to others, as if waiting especially for us to find them.

My friend Susan, for example, had several chances to purchase a highly desirable waterfront property, securing it on her terms nearly a year later. She had already walked away from it twice, thinking it well outside of her means. Meanwhile it sat there quietly waiting, somehow ducking under the radar of other potential buyers. Clearly it was meant for her. The same thing happened to me later, when the time was ripe to find my perfect boat. It called me and I listened.

Even the most left-brained amongst us, will use phrases such as *it was meant to be* or *I just knew it*. These illogical expressions do have meaning to us, regardless of our metaphysical beliefs or non-beliefs. The right word at the right time can wake us up to a new possibility. A meaningful book can appear when we are ready for it and can change our lives. We accept that there are defining moments at certain times of our lives that can set us off in different directions. They are like branches in the road with a signpost on one path that calls us to follow it.

These pivotal moments are rather like gifts that are being presented to us, that we can take or refuse. It always makes me wonder what is going on. And more than that, could things have gone differently? They are opportunities and usually are quite rare. The interesting thing to consider here is this: is it possible to create these opportunities for ourselves, or do they simply happen for no apparent reason, or at least none that we can fathom, measure, predict or control? Bit by bit, very gradually, my life experiences began to have me lean toward the former proposition - that we *can* exert some influence over our destinies. I began to understand that this influence goes beyond the realm of ordinary events, where the likelihood of such coincidences is small, and moves into the extraordinary, where the unlikely can become predictable.

Chunking down

In the pre-planning stages of my business, one of the questions that got the ball rolling was contemplating the rather abstract notion of exactly how many 'widgets' it would take to buy a big yacht. At that point, having absolutely no idea of what a widget might be, I mused on the obvious next piece of information in the equation: "How much does the said 'big yacht' cost?" Knowing that, it then becomes a simple long division sum: "If you divide that cost by the profit from each widget then that's how many you need to sell." Realizing just how do-able the numbers seemed I gave one of those "ah-ha" laughs, the kind that are accompanied by a light-bulb above the head. That was a pivotal moment for me, when the 'penny dropped' and it didn't seem so unattainable any more. A surge of excitement rushed through me as everything suddenly fell into place. Yes! I could clearly see it, from beginning to end. Each step was already there; all that had to be done was take the first one. How hard could that be?

This epiphany of possibility exemplifies the notion of 'chunking down' or breaking seemingly huge goals down into bite-sized chunks, so that they can be accomplished one step at a time. The big picture is usually too large, too overwhelming to contemplate and often stops people from even beginning. Whereas to mentally picture the individual steps, and most importantly, the first step, usually provides enough confidence to begin.

For me, the seed was sown, the outcome visualized, and most importantly, written down in the present tense, as if already here. Within the next few months the seeds began to germinate. My life was about to take the most radical change imaginable, and in an extremely short time. I didn't know this at the beginning, only that I had a part to play that no-one else could play.

A strong inner knowing convinced me of its rightness and of its achievability. The ultimate vision was there to guide me to it, but I still had to follow the path. To me, it was an exciting, unknown territory.

Stepping stones

So began the rewarding journey to find out what works and what doesn't, to learn exactly how to step outside of the norm, how to avoid the pitfalls of the traditional style of running a business, how to explore outside the square and how to fast-track success on all levels. As mentioned earlier, it pays to build on existing skills and resources, and luckily I had a few, even though at the time, I hadn't fully appreciated their relevance to this new venture. This was probably because they came from a different part of my life; one that seemed far removed from the corporate world - and back then, I hadn't fully understood the integrated nature of all these aspects of the whole. Now of course it seems perfectly obvious that this side of things could never be excluded; indeed is the precursor and carrier and crux of everything, the underlying force that pervades every tiny part of life, without which, 'success' would be hollow and meaningless.

There are innumerable ways to make a living but it is most satisfying to make it whilst helping others. This in itself provides additional momentum and incentive for taking a product to the marketplace, knowing that many more people can be reached than within one's own small sphere of influence. While the risks and costs of commercial scales of production are very high, in my own case, I felt it was something I simply had to do. This was not an easy decision and it would be foolish to go into business wearing rose-colored glasses.

Trying to find balance between the various aspects of life is not so simple, and adding the demands of a fledgling new business can be yet another thing to fit into an already pressured schedule. But balance is not so much an attempt to spread equal attention to each facet of our lives, but more about priorities and choices of how we want to spend our time. Working for ourselves can provide that luxury. It is possible to find balance not through a more frenetic juggling act, but through awareness of our priorities and a conscious allocation of our time and resources. This can help us to avoid a sense of panic, thoughts that "there's never enough time" or resentment against things that pull us away from where we think we should be. If we can eliminate the "should be's", it is easier to stay calmer. Later chapters in this book will provide suggestions on how to do this.

Timing is another extremely important consideration in launching any new product. There has to be a demand for it and preferably a growing demand. It's no use making the best possible manual typewriter if no-one has wanted one for at least fifty years. Some people naturally have a good sense, almost an intuitive or sixth sense for what is going to be the next biggest thing out since sliced bread, be it funny shoes called 'Crocs' or internet sites like 'e-bay'. To be at the forefront of such demand is what is defined as true entrepreneurship. You have to be able to see the need first of all. Then comes the hard yakka, the nitty-gritty of the daily grind to make it fly. The generally accepted formula is "ten percent inspiration; ninety percent perspiration". I would change those percentages to include a big dollop of Zen Factor as the primary ingredient. This is the difference that makes the difference, the element of connectedness with everything; where otherwise there are only disparate, often warring parts, anomalous and asynchronous pieces of the puzzle.

Chapter 4

Out on the skinny branches

This is the jumping off point, where you must decide if what you have is good enough to invest in. It is a much bigger gamble than any other, as is evidenced by the fact that banks are always slow to come forward with finance for these new ventures. Generally they will not even talk to you unless you already have something solid behind you that can be used as collateral. 'Bricks and mortar' is the preferred security, but that is not to say they won't consider other things, such as someone else going guarantor for the loan. That person might be a parent or a partner or someone with some vested interest in the business's potential profit who is willing to take a chance where the banks wouldn't. It is also quite feasible to start small, using only your own savings or credit card. There are many sources of capital that you might overlook, such as partnerships, or alliances with existing businesses. The main thing in raising capital to fund a business is having an unbending confidence in its success.

Other sources of capital are what are known as 'business angels' – usually quite wealthy individuals with money to spare who are willing to take the risk for a higher return than bank interest. These people are usually very astute businessmen or women in their own right, with a good eye for potential and a nose for success. They sniff out fledgling businesses that seem to be made of the right stuff, in the same way that they invest in under-valued 'penny-dreadfuls' on the stock exchange. If only one out of ten takes off, it doesn't matter if the others crash and burn. They still come out ahead and no doubt enjoy the ride. Then there are straight out benefactors with a lot of faith in the product or in the service's inherent value and benefit to society. These can be more akin to charitable organizations, willing to support something seemingly worthwhile for humanitarian reasons alone. Their donations provide tax-deductible kudos.

Whichever way, most small businesses will require some initial funding before things begin to gather their own momentum. Once the ball starts to roll, it quickly develops the snow-ball effect, where a small beginning gathers more of the same to itself and becomes a self-perpetuating force. The tiny seed of an idea begins to sprout and the shoots look green and strong. They seem healthy enough to grow all the way into the tree to come. You can picture that tree already. It stands tall and proud with a deeply embedded root system. No storms will topple it.

This kind of vision adds excitement and energy to all who are touched by it. The more people that can be touched and moved to share in an idea, the stronger that idea becomes. A vision that is shared is always more potent than a solo attempt to fly. Mahatma Gandhi rallied his supporters and followers to mount a peaceable resistance force. Jesus Christ had his disciples and scribes to disseminate his teachings to become the mass movement of later Christianity. Ideas may only be thoughts, but these have the power to move mountains. Harnessing this power is what this book is about. It goes way beyond concepts such as being in the right place at the right time, or just being lucky.

Luck can be defined as a kind of happy coincidence, where what we want coincides with what we get. Malcolm Gladwell, in his book *"Outliers: The Story of Success"* wrote that ""Luck" is winning the lottery. Success comes from luck, seeing an opportunity and seizing it." Many of the entrepreneurs studied in his book came from very disadvantaged backgrounds yet found that through seeing opportunity, "using mind and imagination, they could shape the world to their desires."

In many ways we can create our own luck. There are specific tools for doing so and they can be learnt and practiced. It is important to understand that they can only be developed through regular practice. Otherwise it is like giving someone a treasure map and a shovel - completely useless if they fail to ever dig up the buried treasure. It is one thing to have the necessary tools to find success; it is another to use them. The Zen Factor is not an abstract notion but a practical application of specific tools with which you can shape the world to your desires.

Planning stages

"There are literally thousands, maybe millions of things we can do to earn money. Some people have more say in it than others. People who start up their own business have the most say in it. It is entirely their choice, in every way, from what to call it, to how to run it, to when to leave it. It is an act of creation, an extension of one's self. It is built up from nothing and shaped into something. Every step along the way there are decisions to be made that will shape its final form. It is crucial, in the early stages, to contemplate what that final form will be, so it doesn't end up some amorphous blob. Then, like any good sculptor, the decision-making process, where to chip and mould, will be guided by that vision. As is so often said, "Failing to plan is planning to fail." Silly really – as if anyone actually plans to fail. Of course not. But many, many, fail to plan." (Author's personal journal entry.)

In order to convince the banks or any other lender that this is a reasonably low risk venture, it is first necessary to come up with a credible business plan. This shows exactly how much financial assistance is required, what it is to be used for, and how and when it is to be allocated. A good business plan is essential. It provides the template for everything, from set procedures for answering the phone, to how, when and where to advertise. It is a living document that needs to be constantly referred to and amended if necessary. It spells out the goals and vision, the values and ethics of what will become the company. It enables practices to be replicated in exactly the same way, so that high standards of quality control can be assured. It defines when and where changes are to be made to facilitate growth and when and how the final bow is to be taken. Perhaps most of all, it enables others to quickly assess the potential value of the business and if it is worthwhile investing in – if the goals are realistic and achievable and if the yardsticks to measure them are in place.

There are set guidelines for all this with specific frameworks that potential investors recognize and expect to see. No need to re-invent the wheel. I figured the easiest way to get a grip on it all was to attend an adult education short course in small business management. I attended night school along with a handful of other budding hopefuls who benefited from the guidance of a teacher who had been there, done that before us. These days it is possible to get computer programs that walk you through the process of writing a business plan. A few weeks later my masterpiece was done, spelling out in black and white the goals and guidelines, the checks and measures, the fuel and fire of my dreams.

Unification

It felt as if I held the future in my hands when I approached the bank. In many ways I did. On the day of the interview I knew to expect something special. Rather than approaching it with trepidation, I saw it as an opportunity for me to share my enthusiasm with a complete stranger, to let her feel the energy, the excitement, the inspiration and the certainty of success that was within me. It was important to hold the vision of my goal clearly before my eyes and to carry with me an unstoppable determination that spoke volumes in every silence. I had mentally rehearsed beforehand the content of that unspoken attitude that told of humanitarian ideals and the great opportunity to share in it that I was presenting. The assuredness of success stemmed from a future certainty that looked back to this beginning and saw it as a necessary first step in a foregone process. Like building a castle, I was the architect of the dreams that would grow into their already-conceived reality, stone by stone. The right to lay the foundation stone was a privilege that I was offering.

But the plans for a building, a material construction, present a more tangible result than those for a small business that basically hangs on an ephemeral idea, a possibility. How to convey that possibility to a financier, and most often a skeptical one, in only an hour or two of their time? How to have them realize that the idea is the reality and that the means are an integral part of it? In many ways I had to become a kind of modern-day alchemist, transforming clay into fire, darkness into light, vision into form.

These concepts are certainly beyond the everyday experience. It was up to me to create a union between us, a link that allowed for a deeply intuitive, silent sharing. We had to become as one in that moment. It was a union that certainly transcended words; indeed the fewer words spoken the better. Words would only get in the way and cloud the connection that had to be established. This young woman could share my vision and provide the means for its fulfillment, or not. I had never met her before but that didn't matter. Sitting in her small office, taking in the minimal decor designed to hold her to her normal station of major decision-making, we met with an unusual ease.

It was an exceptional meeting, one of those rare events that we so seldom get to experience, where you cannot pinpoint anything specific or tangible afterwards that could possibly explain what happened. But you know that something, something completely beyond the norm transpired, something more akin to magic, if that was a notion the logical brain could allow. The *"Course in Miracles"* tells us to expect miracles, as part of our everyday life, and indeed it is a good way to be.

On that landmark morning, the miracle transpired and we both felt it. I can still recollect the depth of her smile; for want of a better word, it was 'angelic'. She was angelic! Suffused with so much light, it seemed she was almost shining. And as if reciting a prepared script, where the perfect words could not be altered or deviated from in any way at all, she gave me her assurance, as if it was indeed a foregone conclusion: "The fact of the matter is," she told me, "I submit dozens of business loan applications every day. Most get rejected - but you can be certain this one will pass."

Magic! Or was it? I prefer to think it was more to do with the Zen Factor, that intangible force within - something available to every one of us. It is not some clever sleight of hand or act of manipulation. It is recognition of the truth within us, which at its essence is love. It engenders a sense of gratitude and humility, as well as a responsibility as to how we use it. If we can align ourselves with that power we can create our world to be a reflection of it. There are specific ways in which to do this, which I have been graced with the opportunity to use on several occasions in my life and have always witnessed the same miraculous results.

Our potential selves

We need to appreciate that the external world as we perceive it is not a solid, fixed entity, but infinitely malleable and dependent on a great many influences, some of which we can affect. The question to ask ourselves is do we choose to be a cause or an effect? Or as *"A Course In Miracles"* asks: Do we want the problem or the answer? These are not just abstract notions to provoke controversy but signposts toward a deeper meaning that can be experienced directly. When we experience ourselves as a cause in our own world, we are empowered. We are able to affect positive outcomes and to achieve our full potential.

This potential is a latent force lying dormant within all of us. It is available to us through self-realization, through removing the blocks to the awareness of its presence. Whilst we might imagine we know who we are, more often we are basing that identity on superficial things such as our careers, our possessions, or what others think of us. A more accurate reflection of who we are can be found in our inner state of being (still this is only a reflection). Ask yourself the question: Am I at peace within, or am I still reacting like a two year-old child to things that displease me?

As discussed earlier, emotional freedom is lacking when we have involuntary, knee-jerk reactions to outside disturbances. In those moments, we are choosing to value those small irritations more highly than our inner peace (they may seem to be large, yet due to the fact of their impermanence, you can be assured that they are all small). We then choose to give up our inner peace, to deny our potential higher self, to sacrifice unity and love, for small-self immersion in worries, fears and self-righteous judgments. There are practical tools for rising above this immersion.

The Zen Factor is accessed not by airy conjecture but by practical application. Subsequent chapters contain some of the more useful tools for removing the blocks to our realizing this. The phrase "removing the blocks" is a way of saying that what we are uncovering already exists within each of us. No doubt there are as many ways to heaven as there are people. It is helpful to seek role-models, to follow sign-posts of those who have been before and to try out different ways before deciding if this is your way. An eclectic approach is always useful, gathering up various bits and pieces that can be merged into something that feels right and most of all, which works. This is how I have lived my life, exploring, testing, and checking feedback on usefulness. The ultimate test is usefulness. It has to work for you. There are guiding parameters, within which we move and have freedom to choose. To choose freedom, everything we choose must always be in accordance with where we are heading. It must accord with our vision. It must satisfy our deepest needs and provide us with an ultimate sense of peace.

To use an old analogy, as we gather up stones to put in the jar, we must check that they fit with the rest, that their individual attributes are in sympathy and uphold the overall scheme. In starting any new venture, we need first to have a crystal clear notion of what this is. All of this vision has to be there, right at the beginning. It is like a holographic paradigm, where the whole is contained in each and every part, no matter how tiny. There is no part that is too small or too insignificant that it can be overlooked. It is virtually impossible to envision all of this at the outset without having access to the Zen Factor. Too many balls in the air at once and the juggler loses concentration. But when all the balls are really the one and the same ball, it gets simpler. This is the art of it; this is the quiet knowing that underpins every decision. All the balls that might bounce in or out of the picture are here now, in this one ball that is present in this very moment. This can be realized so deeply that it becomes like second nature and everything flows like an unblocked river. It has its own purpose and becomes the guide to its own realization.

Fluidity in motion

One thing that cannot easily be included in the business plan is the Zen Factor. That is something brought in by the proprietor and creator. A potential investor (like the woman in the bank) might recognize it as a high level of energy that is almost tangible and quite contagious. There is a sense of certainty in success that is so strong as to be inspirational. To inspire is to breathe life into something, to transmute it from dull clay to a living entity, a proud and magnificent creation that will be as attractive as a magnetic force. There is nothing more attractive than an unwavering belief in success. The image of that success is so real as to already have its own existence even before it has begun. The goal posts are already in place and the results decided. The rest is simply filling in the gaps, in between now and then, taking the preordained steps that have been mapped in the plan and witnessing the vision becoming the reality.

If the belief is strong enough, the entire universe will bend to accommodate and facilitate the transformation. To hold on to such an unwavering belief requires a degree of trust in the power of this gift, as well as a sense of appreciation and gratitude. This needs to be practiced, as with any new skill. The biofeedback mechanisms we have in place that enable us to walk and talk guide us to our ultimate success. So too, the feedback we receive from practicing the Zen Factor flexes our metaphysical muscles and enables us to develop greater levels of trust and confidence in our ability to affect positive outcomes in our lives.

The Zen Factor can be considered a way of looking at the world in which we are more than a mass of molecules fixed within the boundaries of individual bodies that exist separately from one another. By becoming more aligned with truth, tapping into a higher level of consciousness, we can create our own reality, one in which mind can influence matter. For some people, this concept might rankle, conjuring images of Uri Geller's bent spoons. Closer to home, we can deduce more common causalities, as in the case of sad thoughts producing tears in the eyes, or erotic thoughts giving rise to other physical effects. Mind and body are symbiotically interlinked. It is not too great a leap to extrapolate to other interconnections, communications and spheres of influence that minds might also be able to affect. As with learning to walk, it is not something that words can easily convey - but there are plenty of examples to follow. We can feel our own way, falling and getting up again, or we can take heed of those who have gone before us.

If it could be said that there was a bandwagon that all the sages of all the ages have pushed, the common theme is awareness. The Buddha taught the virtue of mindfulness; Christ asked his disciples to stay awake in the garden of Gethsemane and watch while he prayed but they fell asleep. There is both a physical and metaphysical understanding of falling asleep and awakening. Sadly, most of us live our lives asleep. That is to say, we perform habitual actions and react to the present as if it was the past. What has been before has set up an expectation that becomes a self-fulfilling prophecy of more of the same. This can be seen in the limitations of adults who were constantly told they were clumsy children, or no good at spelling, or would never amount to anything.

A woman I know makes comments like "I could never write a thesis". If she knocks a glass off the bench and her friends say, "Accidents happen", she replies, "Especially to me." Such pronouncements imprison us, keeping us bound to someone else's idea of what we are and what we can be. We are not awake to our present reality and thus can never be truly free of limitations or reach our full potential in life. We are self-sabotaged from the outset, disabled by our own agreement and unaware that it is even so.

Negotiating the maze

It is always the things we don't see coming that catch us unawares and bring us unstuck. So awareness is the answer because without awareness we are blind mice in a black maze. In meditation, awareness is honed through narrowing the object of focus (for example, the breath) and reducing any extraneous distractions. To sit quietly is not something that is easy to do. Many people find this the hardest thing, especially Type A high achievers. But I have seen evidence in stress-management and meditation classes that it is possible for top-level executives to gain enormous benefit from slowing down in this way. Not only do their stress levels drop but their productivity increases and things seem to flow more smoothly in every aspect of their lives.

I was first introduced to meditation in my early twenties through the work of G.I. Gurdjieff, and later went on to explore *"A Course In Miracles"* and other practices, including various types of Yoga, Sufism and Zen Buddhism. Like most people I struggled initially in developing the mental discipline required to quiet the incessant chatter of thoughts that prevent us from reaching that place of stillness deep within us all, but now know it to be well worth the effort. If you find it difficult, my advice is to find a teacher or join a group.

Many analogies have been made in an attempt to describe the meditative state. Some say it is like dropping a pebble into a well and watching for the concentric circles of fading ripples to disappear. My own analogy is of holding the mind like a small bird in the palm of the hand; not so tightly that it is crushed, nor so loosely that it can fly away. Another comparison is with tuning a stringed musical instrument – if it is too loose or too tight it will not produce the right note. So, as with everything in life, it is a matter of finding a delicate balance.

When first beginning a meditation practice, it requires discipline, time and energy from us. But after a while, the practice itself becomes self-sustaining, and ultimately it sustains us, that is to say, it provides us with more energy than it takes. So instead of us feeding it, it is feeding us. Many things apart from food provide us with energy. At that point, there is no struggle against one's so-called 'lower instincts' of idleness because one is drawn like a thirsty animal to water, to drink until slaked. At this point, we open ourselves up to receiving higher energies and to being 'held'. This is a concept that is impossible to comprehend and can only be experienced. When we are willing to take the time out, to give a little time to stopping still, to getting in touch with our deeper selves, there is a definite sense of being supported, in the same way as when we feel loved.

As for the question of how long to meditate each day, my answer is, "until full." It is the same mechanism we (that is, most of us) have when eating food (of the more physical variety), that lets us know when we are done. Providing we have the time and stay aware, we will recognize this satiety. Some days I may meditate for twenty minutes; on others, an hour or more, depending on how much else is going on. If a kaleidoscope of thoughts are whirling around in distracting patterns, just sitting quietly and waiting for them to settle is enough. The length of time devoted to sitting is not necessarily a measure of achievement of a true meditative state. Sometimes an hour can slip by almost unnoticed; other times five minutes can contain such depth as to seem timeless.

Either way, for me, the benefits always outweighed the effort, setting up my days with a calmness that generally enabled me to take things in my stride. If you think of it as extending the 'pain' threshold, meditation helps us to be able to handle greater levels of stress and uncertainty with increased levels of patience and equanimity. We are less likely to be overly reactive to provocation; the old press button A, get response B syndrome. We have choice and we can choose peace.

Awakening

Other positive rewards come from developing a regular meditation practice. These days, our mental states have all been studied, quantified and labeled by modern science. We now know the cycles per second of different levels of brain-wave activity, and even have biofeedback machines to let us know how our meditations are going. As well as that, the physiological benefits have also been recognized and described, from reducing blood pressure to anti-cancer cellular changes. There are many more good reasons for us to 'give up' a small portion of our day to this quietude. Not the least of these is for the practice of discipline. Self mastery precedes mastery of results. If I wish to avoid being pushed and pulled by whatever winds buffet me, if I wish to be a cause in my own life, rather than an effect, I must be able to make decisions that I will stick to. It is no good beginning a new venture if I cannot see it through.

The old saying, "the road to hell is paved with good intentions", tells us that we need self mastery to follow through. Instant self-gratification is a hallmark of our age, along with a reluctance to be uncomfortable. Whenever we find ourselves in an uncomfortable situation, there is an opportunity for us to wake up. We immediately destroy this opportunity through avoidance of the discomfort, for example by laughing or talking to fill in a gap of silence. There are many other opportunities that we overlook because we are too busy to stop for a second. Taking the time to stop and meditate is a form of training in the discipline of awakening.

For myself, I might sit quietly for forty minutes or more before even beginning to enter a true meditative state, especially if I have a lot on my mind that needs clearing. Once there, the state of balance is held effortlessly; there is no effort or struggle; it just is. My sense of awareness of my physical body feels quite different, somehow expanded beyond the confines of my skin. At times there is an inert, almost mineral quality to it. At times it seems my breathing has slowed so much it has almost stopped. The breath breathes itself in and out of my body, as if through a swinging door. The breath connects me to infinity. I can clearly see every thought as it arises and can choose whether to think it or not. I am no longer the thought; I am the thinker. It is from this base that one's life is defined.

"To concentrate your mind is not the true purpose of Zen; the true purpose of Zen is to see things as they are, to observe things as they are, to let everything go as it goes." Shunryu Suzuki, *"Zen Mind, Beginner's Mind"*

Watch the water

Here is a relatively simple starting place that can serve as a useful introduction to developing Zen mind, or no-mind. Sit comfortably, in a cross-legged position or on a chair that can support an upright spine. It doesn't particularly matter where, although it is good to choose a quiet, undisturbed place. If the same place is used regularly it will soon develop its own atmosphere, a peaceful sanctuary from the outside world that is conducive to entering a meditative state more quickly. Preferably sit early in the morning, (pre-dawn is best if possible) for a relatively short period of time, initially perhaps only five or ten minutes but be willing to extend this time as needed. Be as still as possible and pay attention to the incoming breath and then the outgoing breath.

The breath should simply be observed as it is, and not altered in any way. At first it may be difficult not to interfere, but with practice it becomes easier. Simply watch as if you were a disinterested observer, not seeking to gain anything personally. No effort is the way. In the Bodhisattva's words: "In order to see a fish we must watch the water."

When thoughts arise, simply observe them as they are and let them go. It is important not to resist them, as what we resist grows stronger through our resistance.

Also try to avoid getting carried away by them, in the way we commonly recognize as becoming 'lost in thoughts', where several minutes might pass and we are no longer present. It is easy to spot this kind of absenteeism in daydreams, when we might suddenly snap back to the present and wonder where we have been in the interim. While each individual thought may not last long in itself, several thoughts can be strung together in long chains that bind us. So let any intruding thoughts be as they are; acknowledge them, recognize them as being simply waves of your mind, and let them go. After a short while, around ten minutes or so, the endless chatter of the mind is quieted down and the enveloping stillness is held, ever so gently.

Staying present

This meditation is from the Buddhist tradition, and uses the breath as the focus to still the mind. Begin by taking three deep 'cleansing breaths'. These are longer than normal with both the in breath and the out breath being of approximately equal length. Slowly, breathe in through the nose, purse the lips slightly, and then slowly exhale through the mouth. This is a quick way of settling into quietude. Next, attend to relaxing the body for a few minutes, especially the face, which we often unconsciously tense. Observe the large muscles of the thighs, the back of the neck and shoulders and relax them. Once settled, continue to access a deeper quietude, by following your normal breathing at its own pace, as much as possible without influencing it at all.

The breath is mentally observed as it passes the nostrils - but not followed down the airways. Each breath is counted, and the words can be spoken to oneself, to provide a silent 'mantra' or verbal focus to assist in holding the mind from wandering: "breathing in for one, breathing out for one ….. breathing in for two ….. breathing out for two", etc. up to ten. And then repeat, counting the breaths again from one to ten. If the mind wanders it is easy to notice having lost track of the counting. If that happens, begin again from one.

It can be helpful to give oneself some inner guidance at the beginning of your meditation practice, with silent words of encouragement that help define the intent, such as "OK, let's just try and count three breaths". Or if that is too many, "Let's aim for one with 100% attention."

Be kind to yourself with peaceful thoughts like: "Be still" and "Relax". When mind wanders, say gently to yourself, "Come back". In fact, "Come back" is probably the most needed request of self. I often need to ask myself to come back. At times, I am like the disciples in the garden of Gethsemane, falling asleep. Like them, I set the intention of being watchful, I turn to the highest within me, and then in the next second I turn away. But I recognize this without judgment and ask for help to remain attentive. That help always comes.

So at first, do whatever works for you and try out different mental reminders of what it is you are attempting. That way, when your mind goes off track, as it will at first, be your own inner guide, gently remembering your intention and bringing yourself back to it. These are techniques I have found particularly useful in my practice and they make the attempt to count up to ten breaths more achievable.

On some occasions, when particularly distracted by many external concerns, I have not managed to get past the count of one or two. Conversely, I can recollect during at least one particularly deep meditation, that I saw quite clearly that there is only 'One' - only the present breath, being breathed in the present moment. Just as there is effort at first and then no effort, so there is breathing at first, then no breathing as a separate activity. The breath is what connects us to the infinite.

The method is only a means to an end; it is not the meditation. It provides the framework, the rungs of the ladder to climb down, (or "up") into the deeper/

higher chambers of the self. At that point, there is no need to count breaths at all. Here there is no duality of experience, where we might consider "I am breathing". There is no distinction of 'I' and 'breathing'. There is no outer world to draw breath from, nor inner world to breathe into. There is no separation, only a connection to the never-beginning, never-ending.

Such experiences carry over into our daily life, helping us to see things as they are and to stay present to the present moment. The important thing is to be here now. When we are eating, only be eating. When we are washing dishes, only be washing dishes. When we are sitting in meditation, only be sitting. The myth of multi-tasking is an excuse for not paying full attention to now; a diversion that robs us of being fully present in the moment. If we stay in the present, there can be no worries about the past or future. It is much better to let things be as they are and focus attention on just that.

Ultimately each and every moment can become a meditation. This is the ideal state to achieve. It is not a blissed-out, zombie-like state, but one of great mental acuity and keen awareness. There is a profound sense of joy, peace, love, and acceptance. These provide the pre-requisites for an almost background happiness, that resides quietly unaffected by the external highs and lows of our daily life. This equanimity will be of huge benefit when dealing with the obstacles and frustrations that a business owner can encounter. When we are aligned with the higher energy of Life, we can meet each moment freshly, without the preconceptions or preconditioning of the past. There is no need to judge events as good or bad, or to struggle against what is. When we can find peace even in difficulties, when we can let go and return to the events of the present moment, we can be free.

Chapter 5

Removing the blocks

A major part of running your own business involves having to interact with a wide range of people, from work colleagues, business partners, employees, or clients, to the front people of other organizations that either supply goods to us or buy things from us. This is a daily event and one that must be handled with as much integrity and alertness as possible. We cannot be vacant, with our minds elsewhere. How many of us have had the experience of meeting someone for the first time, names are exchanged, a brief conversation takes place, and we walk away asking, *what was their name?* This is a sure sign that we were not present throughout that encounter. Similarly, we might park our car in one of those giant underground car parks whilst our minds are elsewhere and then be unable to find it again later. The frustration of this experience is usually sufficient for most of us to pay attention next time. We know how to do it.

It is particularly important to practice paying attention when meeting people in a corporate setting. Have a mental checklist to focus on, such as: What color shoes are they wearing? What color eyes do they have? How comfortably are they sitting or standing? And be ready to especially make mental note of their name, instantly committing it to memory in some predetermined way, perhaps by association with someone else you know with that name, or some quirky little rhyme. If you miss it, don't be afraid to ask for it again, just as soon as possible. Be real. Admit to a momentary lapse of attention. I am always impressed whenever I come across someone who is able to remember the name of each member of a group of people they have just met. They have obviously practiced developing this skill, which keeps them present, at least during the initial introductions. Everyone likes to be heard.

Engaging

In dealing with others it is evident that quite often our attention is lacking. At those times, we are more concerned with what others are thinking about us, which prevents us from paying full attention to what they are actually saying. Or we are mentally rehearsing what we might say in reply. Or we are a million miles away, thinking about something that happened earlier that day or something we have to deal with later. In these instances, our attention is like a one-way arrow, aimed only outward, or only inward. To be truly present, it needs to be like a double-headed arrow, aiming both inward and outward. Then our focus is neither only on ourselves, nor only on others. Then we are self-aware in as much as we are fully present in the moment, while at the same time we are paying attention and actively engaged with another, in the sense of 'being engaged', like interlocking gears.

This engagement is vital to developing interconnectedness between ourselves, others and our world. In order to be fully present and involved we must first pay attention. When we are open to understand, to share in another's inner world, to delve and explore that wondrous terrain of light and dark, giving it our full attention, we engender trust and loyalty. All of us seek recognition and appreciation and blossom when given it. Everyone knows when this gift is given. When honesty is present, it is safe to be real, to deal with hard topics. This is an area that is often skirted or buried; we hide from ourselves and others, preferring isolation and darkness. In that dim place, miracles can never happen. In isolation we might imagine ourselves strong and capable, but by comparison to the boundless scope of unity, we are helpless. Fortunately there are tools available that can help to forge greater connectedness.

The Power of Sensation

The ability to 'sense' ourselves inwardly is a

powerful tool that brings our awareness back to our centre instead of being scattered and lost in whatever is going on outside of us. It is one of the most important tools we have for quickly raising our vibrations to be in alignment with our higher selves and with the all-powerful, universal life force. In this state we vibrate with a sympathetic frequency that matches the creative energy that empowers us and guides us toward the realization of our dreams. This is impossible to understand with our normal way of thinking. It can be alluded to in creative offerings that move us, such as love sonnets, great art works or beautiful music. The sum of their parts is no measure of their whole and the synergistic entity that is manifest in their beauty is something completely ineffable. It goes far beyond words, paint on canvas or musical notes. It is an experiential knowing that has the taste of perfection or truth about it. We can know these things for ourselves through experience and fortunately others have provided us with paths to follow to reach such realizations. Practice perfection to achieve it.

Sensation is not particularly difficult to practice; it is simply a matter of putting our attention on some part of our body and feeling the physical presence of that part from within. When done properly there will be a tingling that feels a little like mild 'pins and needles' and a slightly increased temperature. Our breathing slows down and the mind becomes clearer, more alert. There is a sense of aliveness and vitality.

Where attention goes, energy flows. This energy is called 'ki' in Japanese, or in traditional Chinese medicine 'chi', and it is regarded as the vital life-force that flows along specific, charted meridians in the body. When the chi is unblocked and flowing freely, we experience the kind of good health that is not simply the absence of illness, but a powerful abundance of energy, as if having tapped into the well-spring of the universal life-force itself. This is the energy that is consciously moved in the practices of tai-chi and kung-fu. We can begin to become familiar with this energy through the use of sensation. This is a basic prerequisite that must be mastered before attempting some of the other techniques described in this book. Fortunately it is not an unnatural addition to our selves, but forms a very basic element of our being that we will immediately recognize like a home-coming. This is the energy that feeds us.

Where are your toes?

At first sensation is best practiced quietly on your own. As in the earlier described meditation, sit quietly with eyes closed, relax and then begin to sense each part of the body in a systematic way. Most people find the hands or feet are the clearest in the beginning. Other parts may be more difficult to get initially, but with regular attention, will begin to respond and open up like a flower bud in bloom. It is as if we are watering the garden of our soul.

If you find it is easiest to start with the hands, hold your attention there for a few minutes. Wait until you get a definite experience of increased warmth and tingling in both hands before moving slowly up the arms, drawing the sensation from the hands up the limb, like a colorful dye gradually suffusing a tube of clear water. If this metaphor is meaningful, choose whatever color occurs to you. If not, stay as strongly grounded in the sensing of the internal limbs as possible.

Join the sensation across the shoulders, then up the back of the neck and over the head to the face. At this stage, it is not necessary to define the separate features such as eyes, nose, lips and so forth, but this will come with practice. In the early sessions, it will be quite sufficient to do only this much and to stay with this degree of sensation for about fifteen or twenty minutes.

Later, continue to sense the rest of the body, again, in a fairly broad, general sweep, down the torso, hips and pelvis, thighs, knees and so on down to the feet. As you get better at it, even each individual toe will become available to you. Once this degree of individuation is possible, it is possible to experience miracles in your life. They might be small miracles at first, such as calming barking dogs, but they will become more powerful with use. It is beneficial to apply the technique in everyday life wherever possible. Practice in small ways at first for only a few minutes a day, such as when standing in a queue at the bank. Rather than feeling impatient or bored or being drawn down worry-lanes, try putting sensation into your hands or feet and notice the difference this makes to your inner state.

Approach this with ease. There should be no strain whatsoever, just a peaceful sense of being present, with a certain 'fullness' inside that feels warm and kindly. Then, instead of getting impatient with those in front of you at the bank who appear to be holding things up, you may notice that they are receiving all the attention they need and know that you will receive the same when your turn comes. You may notice that they need more help than others and feel compassion for them. These new thoughts create a connection with the present and bring you back to remembering your true nature as a peaceful, loving, compassionate, more developed being. Freedom is in this awakening.

Transformations

In the truest meaning, sensation is a link that

joins two minds. When two or more minds are united as one, the possibilities are endless. Later, it can be used in more challenging situations, such as when having to present our ideas to those 'above' us, or to those who seem to hold our progress in their hands (such as the financier at the bank). Invariably, and often seemingly miraculously, they come on-side and are keen to assist in whatever way they can. I have personally witnessed this transformation in many a belligerent CEO who had formerly succumbed to the belief that the only way to rule is through fear. It is quite an amazing thing to see them melt into co-operative, caring souls, willing to share their expertise and guidance in whatever way they can. This is because when we are centered in our own being, we have tapped into a higher power that is recognizable to others. It is a highly attractive and unifying force that makes us one, like the billions of different cells that work together in the one body. There is no fear that one might be better or more special than another. Projecting this oneness into our world, others pick up on it and are inclined to trust us as equally as they would trust themselves.

Confluence

To use an analogy of confluence: picture a small creek trickling down a mountain side through the grassy thickets. Occasionally a miniature dam of fallen branches and leaves might block its course and it relies on being fed by its upstream source to either find a way over or around the obstacle. As it swells and continues, it meets another small creek and they merge in a happy confluence, becoming a larger and stronger stream. Neither resists the union with feelings that its individual identity is lost. Together they do what they were intended to do better, which is to flow along freely. And so they continue, perhaps merging with other streams along the way, to eventually become a mighty, fast rushing river that is even more strongly empowered by the confluence of each contributory. The creek is still contained in the river, at once contributing to and partaking of its greatness. Together, they eventually arrive at the sea and gush gladly into a complete union with that far greater body of potency. Yet the creek still exists, and its individual part continues to play, to meld, to contribute, to be both itself and other, in a way beyond distinction. So too, as we join with others and unite with the greater power of universal intelligence we can enjoy partaking in the abundance of that power.

A word of caution here: it is important not to carry any expectations of personal gain, which can only ever come from a divided space. It is not a case of there being a giver and a receiver, or a greater and a lesser being involved. If you approach situations in this manner, you are bound to fail, because you are attempting to con someone, misusing the power of a shaman or sorcerer. Information is power. To attempt to hide it and hold it for oneself is weakness. The correct way is with love, gratitude and humility, recognizing our essential oneness and knowing that this power is available to all of us and is to bring every one of us to our higher good. Just as you wouldn't attempt to swim the English Channel without adequate preparation, similarly it is important to prepare oneself in advance by developing right mindedness before waving magic wands around. The fact of the matter is that the magic resides in our right mindedness.

As we see it

Projection makes perception, or "as a man thinks, so does he perceive". My father likes to tell a story that exemplifies this. As a young lad living on a farm in the Yorkshire countryside, he had to walk several miles through the snow to the nearest store to buy the daily bread. He knew he had to go; he also realized he could choose how he went – either miserably and feeling sorry for himself, or happily. The choice was his, so he chose to go happily. One of my favorite authors, D H Lawrence, in his novel *"Sons and Lovers"* has the mother say to her complaining son: "If you don't like it, alter it; and if you can't alter it, put up with it." This is not to say keep on grumbling inwardly, but rise above it, embrace it wholeheartedly and make peace with it. The choice is ours. Depressed people are depressing. Bringing a jaundiced view of the world to everything taints everything and builds a "poor me" mentality. This in itself makes us a victim of circumstance and keeps us from experiencing the joy of the present moment. It locks us into suffering, preventing us from knowing our interconnectedness with others and with the universe. From this position, we cannot co-create our own lives or receive abundance. We have turned our backs on our inheritance.

The way in which we choose to interact with our world defines our experience of it, being directly related to what is going on inside of us. First we look within, then without. If our inner world is full of anxieties, fear and confusion and a great many obstacles that seem too high to jump, then that is the reality we will create for ourselves. On the other hand, if we have an awareness of ease and confidence with a strong expectation of success, we will have the Midas touch and everything will flow smoothly. This ease brings with it a sense of inner peace and a certainty that we are on the right track. We are 'in-tune' and in alignment with a higher energy that has its own momentum. It is up to us to choose and this choosing is exercised over and over again, in every moment. Thus we remove the blocks to our awareness of reality.

The Matrix

I have long had the understanding of a 'matrix', a medium in which inter-connected thought-forms exist and within which various patterns can manifest or disappear. An example might be a wave on the ocean, which is constantly changing yet always maintains the pattern of wave-ness. A pattern of possibility is something like a template that holds the form, even when the form is in abeyance. The form of a chicken is latent in the chicken egg, which is unlikely to ever hatch into a sparrow or a duck. When a salamander loses its tail, another one grows into the template of the former tail. The template holds the form which continues to exist invisibly until it manifests again.

The concept of a matrix describes a unified, interwoven grid along which the pathways of existence and non-existence travel as a vibrational force. It may be considered as a medium for cosmic consciousness, within which intelligence/information resides, along with all, as yet, unrecognized possibilities and potentials. Within that medium, vibratory energetic fields move according to various influences, in themselves becoming influences of other effects. Whether we recognize it or not, our thought-forms are part of that influence, helping to co-create the realm of possibility. In this respect, what we think and feel has substance. It is a vibrational energy that we need to take responsibility for.

A more basic example of this is seen in the contagion of moods, where one person's sadness and depression, or excitement and enthusiasm can spread to affect others. Fear is a classic example of such contagion, one that I personally experienced while mountain-climbing in the Alps many years ago. My climbing companion had reached a narrow ledge, beyond which he could move neither up nor down. Prior to joining him on the same ledge, I had been feeling strong and happy, enjoying the glorious day, looking out at the slowly expanding horizon as I ascended. I was like a young mountain goat, completely secure in my own abilities to go in whichever direction I chose.

I could see that my friend hadn't moved for a while, but thought that like me, he was enjoying the view. No words were spoken, yet within seconds of my approaching him, I experienced the same paralyzing fear. We were both immobilized and it took great efforts to overcome this sufficiently to be able to climb back down. I knew without a doubt, it was not my fear, but his that crippled me. I am sure we have all had experiences of similar contagions, when we recognize that we have empathized with another sufficiently to take on their state.

Energy levels, feelings, moods, thoughts, ideas and beliefs all spread along these invisible pathways, creating a pattern of resonance that can be tuned into, rather like tuning into a particular frequency of a radio station. It is this matrix of interconnected intelligence that allows the phenomenon of 'morphic resonance' to occur. This is the term used when new ideas arise simultaneously in different parts of the world, as in the 'hundredth monkey syndrome'. In this example, one or two monkeys discovered that washing their food in the sea removed the gritty sand, thereby making it more pleasant to eat. Soon others followed suit. By the time a hundred monkeys had adopted the new procedure, monkeys on other, distant islands began doing the same. These monkeys had no physical connection or communication with the first group, but had tuned in to the new pattern.

In the same way, 'new' inventions will occur in the minds of thinkers on opposite sides of the globe at the same time. This will be the time when that particular pattern is ready to emerge; it will also be in response to the focus and concentration applied by various minds in that direction. All thoughts are energy. Some are more powerful than others, e.g. those held by a group, like Christians, or Buddhists. Wayne Dyer has written in his book *"The Power of Intention"*: "When you form a thought that is commensurate with Spirit you form a spiritual prototype that connects you to intention and sets into motion the manifestation of your desires."

It's already here

When we exert an influence on our external environment by means of a unified thought form, we are shifting energy closer to being in alignment with the way things are meant to be. That is, there is a pre-existing pattern for all of life that says that the acorn will always produce an oak tree, never an apple tree. When our dreams align with a latency which is possible to manifest, they produce a frequency that exists as a potential pattern that is waiting to be 'discovered', (often by more than one receiver). Tuning into the matrix reveals this possibility and our goals then become a pre-existing template ready to be received. They already exist in the sense that anything we can conceive of does.

Then it may seem to be only a matter of time before those thoughts will manifest into physical form, but as we have seen, time itself doesn't exist independently. As Einstein's theory of relativity has shown, time is influenced by many things, including where an observer is positioned in space. The concept of time serves as a useful convenience but we should not be bound by it. When we apply our imagination to the manifestation of our dreams, there is nowhere and no time that they are not.

Whenever you create anything in time, accept that the only waiting that seems to be involved is derived from our limited understanding of the *isness* of things, which binds us to a belief in process. We are accustomed to believing that consequences follow causes, that events take place in time and therefore when we put a process into action, it will 'move' through time in a sequential fashion. This is perhaps one of the most limiting thoughts we can hold. It prevents us from accepting our freedom, our inner peace and our highest good, right now. The only time it takes is the time you believe it will take. If you believe you need twenty years to get your business running successfully, that thought will create its self-fulfillment – unless of course you tire in the process and think it will take even longer, in which case it will.

Imagination is a powerful tool that is capable of creation and it becomes exponentially more powerful when combined with the more rarified vibration of a higher thought form. Whatever we can imagine must of necessity exist somewhere. It makes itself available to us via our minds, which are infinite in themselves and at the same time connected to the boundless universal intelligence. There are no boundaries to mind just as there are no boundaries to the universe. Through our imagination, we can access all possibilities and perceive of them as already in existence. If you conceive of a time-governed path rather than a fully actualized vision, then that is what you will get: steps along a path to some vague destination. The scriptures sum this up in Mark 11:24: "All things whatsoever ye pray and ask for, believe that ye have received them, and ye shall."

In other words, use all the powers of imagination to create a well-defined goal as if it had already been achieved. Knowing exactly how to do this, is something that several of the tools in this book are designed to reveal. Again, to quote from the scriptures: "For to everyone who has will more be given, and he will have an abundance." (Matthew 25:29) This proverb has had a great many interpretations of its meaning, but you can think of it in the same way as the earlier quotation, meaning that it is necessary for us to first have (create/visualize) our heart's desires, before the actualization of the abundance, which will surely follow.

Ends and means

The goal itself supplies the means for its achievement. That is because our imagination has co-created it, together with universal intelligence, and so it exists in its entirety in the matrix, along with every step that might be taken toward its achievement. There is a greater wisdom that knows each and every step that is an integral part of such a manifestation, but remember that these steps are of your own making. We choose the means at the same time as we choose the goal. The means are co-created as a part of our belief in means and part of our belief in ends. The matrix holds this pattern in the same way as it holds the pattern of the adult that the child will become. It is the way in which the goal is seen that makes the choice of means inevitable.

A well-defined vision that is fully developed from the outset will generate the appropriate means for its realization. If the vision is changed the means will be too. Such is their unity. If the desired outcome can be envisaged clearly at the start and if it is possible to attain, then the means must also be possible. When dreams are conceived and assembled according to a template that contains both function and form, they manifest in their entirety. It is impossible to pick up only one end of a stick. Creation is a holistic manifestation, unified and complete. No parts get left behind. When you envision a well-defined outcome the end result is present in that vision, as is everything that is necessary for its realization. The means are second to the goal. In fact, the means guarantee the goal and are perfectly in accord with it. The universe will bend to accommodate it so that everything falls gently into the right place at the right time. This is the wonder and the miracle of it and the sign of being supported on the way, when we have merged the tiny babbling brook of our small self with the vastness of the ocean.

It is essential to acknowledge this support and to know that of ourselves we are nothing. Each time I sit down to write, a small still voice reminds me, *you will be helped.* I envision that help as guiding my words and the thoughts from which they arise, providing the means to create something that is a reflection of my higher self. In developing my business I was similarly helped and was conscious of that help every step of the way. The vision that I co-created contained all the means for its realization and I followed that path like a devoted servant. I tried not to allow my ego to claim credit for any achievements and always gave thanks at every opportunity. I felt hugely privileged to be granted the tools I used to follow my path. Gratitude and appreciation are vital in being open to receive grace.

Chapter 6

Practicing success

Because perception is a mirror rather than a fact, what we see is a reflection of our own state of mind. If our state of mind is bleak, so too, will be the world we see. Even though our world-view may appear jaundiced, perception depends on our choosing, and we will always choose what we think will bring us happiness. There are times though when we have lost sight of what that might be. That is when the imagination can be utilized to create a new world.

It is known that memory and imagination share the same neural pathways in the brain. In fact, most of our memories are little more than phantasms that we have re-created from bits and pieces of stories and photographic records. The memories I have of early childhood are completely different from those of my brother. His were derived from looking in a different direction, one that didn't even exist for me. From the pieces that captured his attention, he imagined a repressive, unloving family and went on to assemble a safely predictable, mechanistic view of the universe. I escaped to the sea, where it was easier to imagine the exact opposite.

We can use this understanding of the convergence of memory and imagination to great benefit, especially if the beliefs we hold about ourselves and what we can or can't do are based on distorted viewpoints. Mahatma Gandhi said, "Man often becomes what he believes himself to be. If I keep on saying to myself that I cannot do a certain thing, it is possible that I may end by really becoming incapable of doing it. On the contrary, if I shall have the belief that I can do it, I shall surely acquire the capacity to do it, even if I may not have it at the beginning."

Looking back to Now

Everyone can conjure up an imaginary time-line of their life from beginning to end. For some, it runs from left to right; for others, the opposite way. Some people see it out in front of themselves while others imagine it running right through their bodies, with the body standing in the present moment. Interestingly, each of these different perspectives reveals something about how the person relates to time; whether they are the kind of person who is 'in time' or 'out of time' will affect whether they are usually punctual or tardy.

For the 'Looking back to now' exercise, first of all prepare a long scroll of paper with broad time increments written on it, beginning at birth and extending to a possible date of death. It doesn't matter when the end is projected, even a hundred years or more off, so long as it is there. Remembering the finality of that inevitability can alter how we regard our life now. Gurdjieff suggested that we live our lives as if the angel of death was sitting on our left shoulder as our most trusted advisor. When we deny the inevitability of death and the impermanence of everything, we cannot live our lives fully.

Most of us live as if we were immortal, though not in the spiritual sense. We barely give a second's thought to the fact of our physical death. Death is generally hidden from view in our society and mostly regarded with fear or denial. We push it out of mind, regarding it as something that happens to others, not to us. If we did stop to consider the reality of our physical impermanence, we might make different choices in the present. Certainly the minor and petty concerns that can so easily upset us might not seem so big or so worth fighting over. Once again, it comes back to perception, or how we look at it. There are ways of looking at things that cause us suffering and alternative ways that bring a sense of harmony, unity and peace.

It is possible to reframe our world-view by changing our minds, letting go of distressing thoughts and entertaining other, more kindly interpretations of events instead. It pays to stop and ask "is there another way of looking at this?" Switching to more of a "cup half-full" rather than "cup half-empty" attitude is done with the realization that there isn't actually any cup at all, only the attributes we ourselves give to it. Sometimes cups appear hugely important in themselves, quite capable of overturning our world and devoid of any 'silver linings'.

Looking back on now from the viewpoint of our final curtain can provide a new perspective on things and help sort the trivia from what's more important, and even further, separate this from what's most important, namely our higher purpose. We have been granted a tiny allocation of time and space to occupy whilst in this particular embodiment and there are some important tasks to be done while here. There are many ways in which we can find out what these are and begin to implement them.

Purpose provides focus, meaning and a big-picture approach that is capable of overlooking small aggravations. It moves ahead smoothly like a funicular railway carriage on a well-greased track with a strong cable pulling it upward from above. So too our goals pull us toward them, with each station along the way already in place. If we imagine ourselves as already being there, the means will be provided to pull us toward that destination and the tracks and engine will pre-exist as the appropriate form for the function. So it is essential to begin from the end.

A blank slate

Goal-setting is normally done the other way, from the present into the future. But that tends to take the present situation as the starting point and doesn't allow for any quantum leaps into unknown territory. The excitement of life is fed by a blank slate that is replete with infinite possibilities. The goals we set can be as wild as our imaginations can dream up and are most liberating when free of the constraints of the past. The limitations of what has been before need not tie us to a continuation of more of the same; such constraints can easily fall away when we project forward into the realm of open possibility. Sit down with pen and paper or a good friend and conjure up your heart's desire.

Projecting ourselves to a future in which we have already achieved our dreams, then looking backwards, asking how we got there, fills us with wonderment and curiosity. Like small children, our minds are naturally curious and questioning. It is only when we think we know things that we close off the possibilities of learning. Then our cup is too full to allow for anything further to be added. We have grown redolent and complacent, resting on the laurels of repetition and habitual behaviors. The years of living have largely been unguided, uninspired and uninspiring; just a long continuum of more of the same, with no real freedom to even begin to know who we truly are or what we are here for. We are so restrained by what has been and what we believe is or isn't possible, that we scarcely dare to dream of something else. Daring to dream and daring to live our dreams requires self-enquiry and a willingness to question all of our fixed assumptions that we cling to as if they were some vital part of us.

The fact is that what we actually do know is so limited, so bound by our past conditioning, that we can hardly be said to know anything at all. It is useful to remember this when we start thinking something can't be done. Indeed it cannot be done when we put our attention on lack, rather than on abundance, focusing on what's missing, what's needed, what we don't have, and what we can't do. Try letting go of these limiting thoughts, questioning each one as it arises with the thought: '*really?*'

It is possible to nip limiting thoughts in the bud and replace them with limitless ones. Take the opportunity to get playful. Be a cheeky schoolchild who questions everything, challenging the system. We have been trained to fit in, whether we be square pegs in round holes or not, but that doesn't force us to be witless forever. As mature, developed beings, we have the liberty to examine the conditioning of our minds and to step over it. We can sing and dance internally without fear of looking a fool or being made to sit sensibly so as not to disturb others. In our thoughts, we can play out as many wild scenarios as we can dream of as being possible for us to attract into our lives. It is not necessary to shout out loud, although sharing our visions can fuel their fires. Excitement and enthusiasm gather momentum to move and inspire all who come into their energetic realm.

Once you have imagined a life you love, with all the energy of creation ready to create it, the hard part is over. Now, it is time to use the 'Looking back to now' exercise to manifest it: The paper scroll is laid out on the floor (hopefully the room is long enough). Significant events along the way, such as graduations, new jobs, weddings, births, deaths and so forth, can be briefly written in. This past section is not the focus of the exercise, even though it can provide an interesting overview. It is the space ahead, between 'Now' and 'Death', that is of most interest. This portion stretches out before us as a blank sheet - an unknown, empty possibility. Anything at all can be written in there.

Dream weaving

Most people will have some vague idea of what they want from life, if not a burning desire for something in particular. Use your imagination to dream up anything at all that calls you forth, remembering that you are here to become more fully you. Take some time to dream outside the square and write down on a small card a brief outline of that dream, writing it in the present tense, as if it already exists. This can be used as a starting point which you take with you, walking out along your paper scroll, to a place further down the track.

If you think of the time-line as going from point A (birth) to point B (death), walk in the direction of B, stopping at some point in between. It doesn't need to be exact. This is the point at which your goal has been achieved. This is the starting point to begin from – standing in nowhere, in no time and no place. Where anything at all is possible. This is the end at the beginning. Here, your dreams are made real and everything you imagined has come to pass. This is it. You have made it!

Once standing in that future place, breathe in the feeling of success and let it imbue every cell of your body. Let it merge deeply within you; become as one with it, and see there is no separation, either of time or place. It is here and now. It is important to use all the senses to describe exactly what it would be like to actually *be* this experience of success - how it feels; how it smells, tastes, what sounds would be heard and how it would appear to others. Especially consider, how would others see you?

Imagining yourself as seen through the eyes of others is important in creating a fully realizable vision. Jean-Paul Sartre said we can only know ourselves through the mediation of another. Who or what would we be if living in a vacuum? Our goals serve much more than satisfying our own personal gratification; they serve to define us in relation to others. Just as the Dalai Lama's goal is to attain omniscience for the benefit of all sentient beings, so we all need that element of others in our goals. An enlightened hermit who has spent years meditating in a cave must eventually emerge and share his truth with others. A message is only such when it is received.

Having projected yourself 'forward' on your time-line, stand for a few minutes experiencing your desired goal as if it was already achieved. Reaffirm what it feels like, looks like, sounds like, smells like, tastes like and looks like to others. Take a few deep breaths. From this point, look back along the time-line and imagine what might have happened to fill in the blanks. You can then begin to think of the steps you took along the way to reach the fulfillment of your dreams.

The questions to ask are: "how did you get here; what were some of the steps along the way that led to this point in time? What did you actually do? Who was with you? What help did you need? How long did it take to get here?" (Remembering that 'here' is someplace off in the 'future'.) It can help to have another person assist in this questioning, though the answers are only of any importance to you, and don't need to be recorded. The more clearly the process can be described, the better. Remember to turn up the dial on excitement and enthusiasm. It is exciting to achieve your dreams and it is energy that fuels the engine. So imagine how fantastic you feel, being in that successful position that is like a mirror, reflecting creative energy and lighting your way. Think of other times in your life when you achieved something wonderful and remember how good that felt.

Then take a small step backwards towards 'Now', still facing towards point B, with sights set on the projected goal. This new position can be defined as the penultimate step in the process, the point just before reaching the goal, where the goal is in sight and clearly within reach. It is just a short step away; the aroma of success is still wafting around, as tempting as freshly-baked bread.

Again stand still for a few moments here, using all the senses to describe it and getting a strong feel for the imminence of that ultimate position, a position that is now as familiar as yourself. Feel the strong magnetism of it, how it attracts you and pulls you into its warm embrace. Feel the inevitability of it and know that you are not alone here; there are far greater creative forces than those of your small, limited self, that are causing this to be. The resultant manifestation is a co-creation that functions synergistically and ineffably, with all the power of the universe available to drive it. The steps you take are guided in their perfect unfolding.

The first/last step

Continuing to move back toward the present, all the stages of the journey can be charted, stepped into and experienced in vivid recreation. Perhaps the most important is the last step, the step just before stepping back into 'Now'; (if you like, this can be considered the reverse penultimate). Looking forward, this would be the first step that begins the journey. But unlike most first steps, which are often the hardest to take, this one is different. In a sense, it is the last step, rather than the first. Having been approached from the other end, it already has a 'history'. It doesn't matter that this was created by the imagination. As we have seen, imagination and memory share the same neural pathways; therefore it exists as if it had already happened. It has a palpable energy connected to it. It is an undeniable effect of co-creation, with its pre-ordained pattern extant within the matrix.

Stand a while longer in this position. Again, recreate it fully using all the senses. Try to get a strong sense of its inevitability, as if it truly is the second-last step in a series of steps that have all been taken. If your logical brain insists on interposing time frames, supply one and let it travel in whichever direction you want. Do you want it to bring your dreams forth within the next/last two or three years? Or can you accept that your dreams are here and now, as yet unmanifest but ready to become so in time? What, after all, is time? Some scientists now think that time can indeed be reversed and travel backwards. Consider again Einstein's theory of space-time, which is not only relative to the observer but furthermore, curved or warped back on itself by the matter and energy in the universe. In Stephen Hawking's words, "our concept of time has changed from being independent of the universe to being shaped by it." So don't let old-school physics limit your thinking of what is possible.

The dreams we create that are in alignment with the life-affirming force of the universal creative energy are ours to enjoy. Life is abundantly rich, ever expanding through creation. Through the power of our minds, we link with the source of all creation and are simultaneously uplifted to resonate at a higher vibration than our physical selves would decree. Co-creation brings a transformation of both ourselves and our world. Once the transformation is complete, the materialization of our dreams is a foregone conclusion. There is nowhere and no time that it isn't.

All that remains is to feel the pull of the goal to itself and to be hugely thankful for the abundant creativity of life that you are a part of. Every possible moment, give thanks, in the clear certainty of the existence of this desired outcome that beckons you to it. The projected goal has become like a magnet with a power of attraction so strong that it is irresistible. It has an existence in exactly the same way as any of our other projected perceptions. We have projected its possibility out there into our world. We have seen it, smelt it, tasted it and recognized its being. All the molecules of our own being are in alignment with this new creation. It is a part of us. There is no need to whip up any motivation to take that first step. It has already been taken.

Chapter 7

Beyond limits

The catch-cry of the millennium is sustainability. We are better informed than ever before on climate change, global-warming, carbon-sinks and the Kyoto protocol, and what each of the first world governments is doing, or not doing about it. And of course what we ourselves are doing or not doing, in our own small way, which is probably much more significant because there are many more of us. As a small-business owner there are even more opportunities to make more sustainable choices. We can opt for recyclable packaging and advertising materials. The products we make can be bio-degradable, free of petro-chemicals, animal derivatives or harsh detergents. People in general are now much more aware of these things and voting via their purchase preferences for more environmentally-friendly goods and services. They are even willing to pay a bit more to have them, in the recognition that it is a small price to pay to contribute to easing our planet's burden. Each and every one of us has a responsibility to do what we can in this regard.

An illusion of wealth

As one of the relatively poorer members of society and therefore much less of a consumer, I felt that my own contribution to pollution was minimal. I had spent enough time as a single parent to feel hunger as well as the desire to provide more for my four children. I had known what it was like to go on an outing and not have enough spare change to buy them a bottle of water each. It's not an easy place to be, but despite that, we were, for the most part, happy and healthy. I knew how to make wholesome meals inexpensively and how to grow healthy children who knew they were loved and valued. The 'illusion of wealth' was something I always tried to create for my family, scrimping on small things in order to lash out occasionally on bigger things, as if we had plenty to spare. This make-believe abundance no doubt contributed to its later materialization, when it moved from being only an illusion to an actively defined goal. Begin by creating as-if it was already here now. Live *as-if*.

I have always seen the value of education and especially of getting some sort of a qualification, despite my father's rather archaic view that girls didn't need one; he argued it would be wasted on them as they would most likely get married and have children. His prediction for my life was that I would be "barefoot and pregnant" before the age of twenty, "just like my mother". (In fact this did become a self-fulfilling prophecy, as so many of those parental expectations can). I held onto my dreams regardless, wishing I could go to University, become 'something', write books and be the first woman to circumnavigate the globe. Unlike Kay Cottee or Jessica Watson, I hadn't heard about sponsorship; or perhaps it hadn't been so readily available back then. Now it seems ironic that these women sailed around the world to make a million, whereas I had to make a million to sail around the world!

Leaving school and home at sixteen I soon learned that the better educated you are, the fewer hours you have to work to attain the same lifestyle. My first job in a fish and chip takeaway didn't provide much in the way of spare time or cash. When you look around it's not hard to see that unskilled laborers have a much tougher time of it and are usually the first to lose their jobs in a recession. I always drummed the importance of this into my children from an early age, and set the example, studying by correspondence to gain access to higher education. It was a busy time, juggling parenthood, working by day and studying at night. But I was doing something I enjoyed; something that was more meaningful to me, and this kept me committed.

Problem solving

The commitment and perseverance that comes from doing something meaningful is what drives a business through its hard times. There are endless decisions to be made each day and problems to be solved. M. Scott Peck in *"The Road Less Traveled"* has observed "no problem can be solved unless an individual assumes responsibility for solving it." He speaks of the importance of problem-solving as part of our self-development, noting that we set school-children problems to solve in their daily lessons, not so much to get right answers, as for the development of problem solving skills. As we progress through the education system, this is often confused with simply getting the right answer, so that later in life as adults, we generally seek to avoid the pain of problems and often see them as being caused by others. That is, we hide from taking the responsibility and adopt a victim mentality.

Being in business we must face up to this responsibility. One very useful way of doing so, is by setting ourselves small daily tasks to accomplish. If we can train ourselves to do this much, to form an agreement with ourselves that no matter what else crops up in our day, we will accomplish this one thing, we develop the discipline to solve bigger problems. By taking responsibility for our choices, we develop the inner freedom that comes with mastery of self. We acknowledge that we have chosen what we have of our own free volition, not through the coercion of others or our past conditioning. Knowing this, we own our choices, which automatically gives us the freedom to change them if we so desire.

Which shelf?

In business, everyone chooses a sector of the market to aim at, being bottom shelf, top shelf or somewhere in between. To some extent, that divides the market into different playing fields. I decided on the top shelf, providing a top quality product that was made from only the best ingredients available. The costs of production are higher, and generally, the volume of sales lower. If you sell a hundred items for ten dollars, or a thousand items for a dollar the return is the same. In the latter case, the handling may be a lot more, which means more man-hours and perhaps more staff. I wanted to keep those overheads as low as possible.

Costing the product is an interesting exercise. There are many factors to consider, such as how many middle-men will be standing in the line with their hands out. Distributors, wholesalers, retailers - each of these will add their percentage to the final shelf price. And what happens when the business grows and needs extra staff and bigger premises? Can the initial profit margin cover that? These are all things to work out in advance and to include in the business plan. A rough rule-of-thumb is that the cost price should be approximately 10% of selling price.

It is important to know the difference between margin and mark-up. Some distributors or wholesalers will talk mark-up while you are talking margin and the difference is in their favor. Margin is a percentage of the selling price; mark-up is a percentage of the cost price. They are both calculated in a similar way, dividing gross profit by either sales (margin) or by cost (mark-up) and multiplying by 100 to get a percentage. These days, this basic information can easily be found on the internet. Many electronic accounting programs will also cover these topics and some will make calculations automatically for you. It is a good idea to buy one of these programs and learn how to run it. Keeping accurate financial records is vital for providing the major performance feedback of net profit, or how much is left in your hand after all running costs have been deducted. This tells you whether you can continue to stay in business or not; or at very least if the balance sheet is regularly showing figures in the red, that some major changes need to be made.

The spice of life

When I was in private practice as a Naturopath,

I was aware of the fact that there is a subtle matching process takes place between practitioner and client. There needs to be a certain ease and rapport established before the mutual aim of healing is reached. We naturally feel more comfortable with those whom we feel are similar to ourselves. Then there is a bit of shuffling of the deck and a selection process that goes on in the background before we agree to work together. If one client finds another practitioner who suits them better, it is no loss to me. My goal is not to 'take hostages' but to facilitate healing.

It is the same with all the various products out in the market place. Some products will work better than others, for some people. Some people will swear by something their mother swore by and never budge from it; some are willing to try anything new that crops up. Variety is the luxury of a large enough marketplace. We have come a long way from Henry Ford's early automobile, when you could have any color you wanted, so long as it was black. I appreciate the different colors, the different flavors that suit different tastes. In many ways our competitors are our allies, keeping us on our toes, as well as keeping the public aware of the availability of products that may help them. We are all connected.

The body-mind

Naturopaths are trained to view health

holistically, which is to say they aim to treat the whole person, rather than simply focus on the particular manifestation of dis-ease, or unwellness that the person may present with. The interconnectedness of mind, body and spirit is acknowledged and taken into account in any treatment protocol. We cannot ignore the role of emotions, hormones, nutrition, attitudes, values and beliefs or random neuronal discharges. What used to be considered the CPU or central processing unit, the brain, contains 100 million billion billion particles - far too many for us to even begin to understand the capabilities or effects of. We can be certain we only use a fraction of its full capacity.

In the early 1970's, Candace Pert, a neuropharmacologist at the John Hopkins School of Medicine, coined the acronym PNI for Psychoneuroimmunology, to describe how the immune system is linked to a person's emotional and mental states. She wrote "I can no longer make a distinction between the brain and the body". Indeed it seems that thoughts do not even arise in the brain, which is just the hardware for electrical impulses. A more accurate view is to consider the brain as a receiver, capable of tuning into ideas. The physical body used to be regarded as simply a machine. This mechanistic view failed to take into account the innate intelligence evinced, for example, in self-healing.

When we cut our finger slicing beans, within a few days it will have healed itself completely.

Intelligence can be said to reside in every one of our billions of cells, each of which knows exactly how to do its specialized task as well as how to share information with the whole. A new concept of the "bodymind" emerged, showing the impact of non-physical stressors arising from negative thoughts and feelings on the immune system. It was found that people are much more likely to get sick when they are unhappy or depressed, conflicted or in turmoil. A sense of not being in control of one's own life is seen as one of the biggest contributors to this. It is not uncommon to see people who hold onto a victim mentality, believing that bad stuff just happens to them and that there is nothing that they can do about it, succumbing to illness and depression. They are an effect, rather than a cause in their own lives.

How often do we see someone who has taken on more than they can handle become ill? This might manifest in small ways at first, such as the occasional headache or upset stomach, which is seldom associated with the actual reason behind it. In some peculiar way, we seem to overlook any part we might have played in the choosing of our higher stress levels and instead feel we are the victim of some unrelated ailment. We have a dozen different reasons at the ready to explain why what is must be as it is, and why we are stuck with it. We fail to ask ourselves is this of my own making. Am I looking at the problem instead of the answer?

A definition of insanity

When there are too many things going on at once, the demands of modern life can seem overwhelming. Most of these things are unseen and not real. For example, a businessman with an important meeting scheduled, might worry over how the day will pan out. Such thoughts produce considerable anxiety, even though none of the actual challenges is present right now, or even certain to eventuate later. Very often, what may or may not occur creates a greater sense of dread than what actually does occur. The businessman may justify his concerns based on prior experience; he knows what these meetings are like! However, this is allowing the present to be dictated by the past. This perpetuates a most-likely future and doesn't allow an opening for any new possibility to happen instead. A definition that I like of insanity is "keeping on doing the same things and expecting to get different results".

The fact is that when challenges are happening in the present moment we tend to deal with them as best we can. It is not the problem of the moment that causes the ulcers, but the worry over those that have occurred in the past or those that are yet to come. So it is important to develop the ability to stay present to the present. This ability is a direct result of training the mind to be more disciplined in its mental maneuverings, keeping a sharp lookout for disabling self-talk.

What do we think about? Is it helpful or not? If not, why are we thinking about it? Can we let it go and choose not to think about it? Have we found the switch-track (or switch-off) button? To be immersed in a business of one's own requires this kind of discipline. Otherwise worries will take over the mind and the great "what if" will lay its eggs in the fertile muck of anxiety: "What if this should happen, or what if that should happen?" Uncertainty will undermine the initial determination and clarity of the novice entrepreneur. This is best avoided through meditation and written goal-setting. The clarification of the goal belongs at the beginning of any enterprise, for it is this which will determine the outcome.

The Outcome Meditation

The Outcome Meditation is another powerful and valuable tool. It is a direct line to the future, ensuring the success of whatever goals are set. The future can be considered an extension (or expansion) of now, so now is the only time we have to affect any change. If we wish things to be different in the future we must do something about it now. Otherwise we will get more of the same, forever stuck in the old self-perpetuating loops and patterns. Now is the only time we have to work with. But we must be vigilant and watch ourselves closely, uncovering each and every mind-set that would keep us hostage. It is only because we don't fully appreciate the power of our minds that we leave them so unguarded and wayward. Thoughts are energy and they create energetic fields that have far reaching effects. If we could appreciate the magnitude of the energy-fields that our minds are capable of producing, and see their effects, we would be much more careful.

In the disciplines of tai-chi and kung-fu, energy-fields can be shifted from within and without, harnessing the more potent forces in a unified field; so too in the Outcome Meditation we can utilize this technique. The energy can become like a familiar friend that can be felt and seen and played with as it is flipped from inside to outside the body, until there is no distinction, and the energy simply is.

In this meditation, we can experience the realization that time is only a social convenience that does not travel a linear course, or even remain constant. In Einstein's fourth dimension of space-time, the 'isness' of now becomes present. What has been before is also present, as is what is to come. Just as in the meditation that counts the breath and then sees that there is only this one breath, so too, there is only this one moment. And if the desired outcome is created powerfully now, it is here already.

The swinging door

So once again, sit quietly in a quiet place, close the eyes and turn within. Take a few moments to still the mind. Three or four slow, deep cleansing breaths are conducive to this. It also helps to roll the closed eyes back in the head as if looking up at the inside of the skull for a few seconds, and to touch the tip of the tongue to the roof of the mouth for as long as is comfortable. Relax the body as much as possible, especially the muscles of the face and the large muscles of the thighs. Feel yourself sinking more deeply within, becoming quieter, more in tune with that deep reservoir of tranquility.

Then think of the desired outcome, saying to yourself, "I am setting the outcome that ...." - and state the goal as if it had already transpired. Spend a couple of minutes visualizing the outcome, and then let it go.

Then begin a process of shifting the consciousness

from within the body to without and vice versa. Start at the top of the head and work the way down the body in a systematic order, from top to bottom and from front to back.

At each part, say to yourself, "I am seeing the top of my head from outside of my body" (at first, use the imagination to 'see' it in your mind's eye). Then shift your attention to an internal view and think, "I am sensing the top of my head from inside of my body" (and then draw your attention inward to sense that part, using the power of sensation that you have already learnt). Imagine a swinging door, with attention flowing from the outside to the inside and then back out again. As always, no effort is the way.

This flipping in and out can be done quite quickly, say over a breath or two. It doesn't need dwelling on. Don't try to do it perfectly; it is enough to direct your attention/energy via the intention to do so. Eventually, it will become much clearer.

Next, move away from the top of the head, bringing your attention forward and down the front of the body, saying to yourself, "I am seeing my face from outside my body." (this should be a little easier, as we have all seen our own face in a mirror, so can more readily picture its features). Hold that image for a short while as it develops, then flip your attention inward again, thinking "I am sensing my face from inside my body." It is not necessary to sense each facial feature separately, such as the nose, eyes, mouth, etc., but if they present themselves as being available to you, allow that to be.

Then move at whatever pace and in whichever increments feel right to you, perhaps down to the neck, observing: "I am seeing my neck from outside my body" and then "I am sensing my neck from inside my body."

And so on, down to the feet and then returning up the back to the top of the head again. You can choose when and how to move down the trunk, the arms, the hands, possibly each of the fingers; then the pelvis, the genitals, the legs, feet and toes. Similarly, you can choose whether to scan externally or internally first, whichever suits you best. I personally prefer to envisage the outer aspect first, before sensing each part from the inside, but occasionally I change this just for flexibility. The order is not important either, and you can either scan down the front of the body first, then proceed up the back, or from back to front. There is no need to scan the internal organs of the body, such as the liver or pancreas (indeed, most people have little concept of the location of such parts, or what they would look like.) So just stick to the externally visible parts, such as arms and legs, but do concentrate on sensing these parts from within and hold that sensation as strongly as possible.

At first this may be difficult to achieve, but with practice it will become easier. As mentioned before, the hands and feet are generally the easiest to sense from within. There is a tingling sensation as if more warmth or increased blood flow had gone there (which indeed it has). By now you will be familiar with this experience that 'energy flows where attention goes'.

Once back to the starting point at the top of the head, picture the entire body from without, and simultaneously sense the whole body from within. As you sit like this, hold the sensation of the whole body as strongly as possible. Allow it to spread and grow in intensity. Such powerful sensation produces a profoundly altered state of consciousness, in which the physical body seems to almost disappear. Then reiterate the intention, as if it already exists, and sit quietly for a few minutes more. After the meditation is finished, write the intended outcome down using the present tense. It will be much more powerful then, rather than writing it down before doing the meditation.

This is one of the most powerful tools available, and I have never known it to let me down, whether I am using it to manifest small or large outcomes. Even an imperfectly executed Outcome Meditation brings results far more rapidly than no meditation. Start small if you wish, but start. Buy a beautiful new notebook and write down your goals in the present tense, describing in as much detail as possible, what you already have, as if you already had it. Remember, never ask for what you haven't, as this is what you will get. Always create as if you already have it. Then surround yourself with things that support that reality and act as if it were here and now.

Delimit your dreams

One of my early outcome meditations stated that, "Within the next two years, I have half a million dollars in the bank." I was rather shy of this one at first, thinking it too pecuniary and ambitious. I had absolutely no idea of how this was going to materialize; or whether it was in some way unsavory to set a goal with a certain monetary value. We all have preconceived notions about money, just as we all have what is known as a 'glass ceiling' that prevents us from rising above the level we think we belong to. It is extremely difficult for poor people to rise above their station in life, not because of external circumstances but because of how they see themselves and where they fit in.

It is best to be as specific as possible in setting the goal and to make the declaration in the present tense. It must be as if it is already here, in existence, right now. Otherwise it will be like asking for things you don't already have, which is what you will get – nothing. To ask for things, like money or love, is to convey a message of lack. It comes from neediness and insufficiency. The only way to manifest our goals is to create them now. Then they can reveal themselves to us, along with all the means for their realization.

Don't be afraid to aim high. (In fact, as it turned out, I was being rather conservative). A good idea is to delimit the goal by adding the words, "or less" for the time-frame, and "or more" for the number of zeros following the one – if your goal has a numeric value, that is. Then the universe can open up its storehouse of abundance in unlimited measure. As the good book tells us: "Ask and ye shall receive."

SECTION II

BUILDING YOUR DREAMS

Chapter 8

Expansion

"We are climbing steeply now, up a very sharp incline. The stakes are higher, and so the attendant risks also increase. In stretching and reaching for more than I ever thought possible there is the risk of losing it all, even the little bit that I started with. It is at once exhilarating and terrifying. What if I fall? Of course this question must be asked and the worse-case scenario considered. Nothing. Consider that for a moment – nothing. To go right back to the bottom, like in the game of snakes and ladders. To have climbed so far and then to fall. But just as to have everything brings its own costs, so too does having nothing bring its positive side, one that I have been very familiar with. It becomes clearer now, to understand true detachment and equanimity." (Author's personal journal entry.)

In a short while, I found my role was shifting to one of education and marketing. I was only spending one day a week in clinic as a health practitioner. This is a common scenario, (as described in the book *"The E-Myth"*), where the hands-on carpenter or pie-maker lay down their tools and become the entrepreneur. It is a shift that a lot of people don't feel quite comfortable about. They are used to seeing themselves as a plumber or tiler and that is how they define themselves. They are not happy being the Director or CEO. They may have preconceptions about what that status infers. Or they simply feel unequal to the role. For some the leap is too great and they set about subconsciously sabotaging themselves.

This is where self-awareness can help. Through questioning our motives and our actions we can discern patterns of negativity. Whenever things are not flowing smoothly it is always a sign that we are out of sorts with ourselves. It is time to get back in touch with our inner guidance, to take some time out from our busy schedules to look within. There is no other way of calming down more quickly and resolving any problems than to sit in meditation, just following the breath. I personally had many frustrations and set-backs that provided me with opportunities to do this. My outer world was colored by certain fixed ideas that I held onto as if they were an important part of me. To question these is to question our identity, yet they must be questioned before we can advance.

As we have already learned, projection makes perception, in that it first selects what we believe we know from our past experience, and then creates the world we see. It is highly selective. If ten different people were to witness the same accident, there would be ten different versions of what happened. First we judge, then we project that externally, then we see what we have judged. The rest we are blind to. 'Reality' as we know it is just a symbolic extension of our past. It is always our past preconceptions that cause trouble in the present. In any situation, there are two components: the 'what happened' and the 'story' we make up about it. It is usually the latter that stays with us and becomes our cross to bear.

Contemplating this deeply meant facing a lot of old 'stories' that I had been carrying for a long time and feeling the dead weight of them upon me. Like for instance the broken record that had been endlessly spinning about "my mother deserted me when I was two years old." It is easy to spin these webs into cages with steel bars that imprison us for life. We form set beliefs about the world and how we are to be in it; what is safe and what is dangerous; who to trust and who to avoid. Most decisions we make as adults are based on the fears of a two year-old child. As we see it, so it is.

Change your thoughts and you change the world. Just like the young Yorkshire lad plodding happily through the snow, it is a case of mind over matter - if you don't mind, it doesn't matter. Shakespeare said that "there is nothing good nor bad but thinking makes it so". Facts in themselves do nothing. This idea can even be extrapolated to state that facts in themselves are nothing. How can we begin to believe in the existence of an objective reality, when so many of us apprehend it differently, when every one of our own senses can be so easily deceived? If we consider each of the senses, and ask ourselves has there ever been an instance when what we thought we saw or heard was 'wrong', we realize these perceptions are not infallible. Does the camera lie? Can graphics be manipulated? Can sounds be distorted? Can 'truth' be distorted? Engineers have a saying: "believe nothing of what you hear and half of what you see." More likely our interpretation will be based on our expectations, conditioning and preconceptions. The one thing we can change is our mind.

Getting help

The sole trader soon reaches the point where they can no longer continue to run the show on their own; they need help. Even if outsourcing most of the jobs, such as manufacturing and distribution, the paper-war mounts to the ceiling, the phone keeps ringing and emails need answering. The Director's role becomes more one of liaison, or the 'glue' that binds all the outsourced help together. At very least an in-house secretary or office-manager is needed. A part-time book-keeper and maybe a storeman/packer would be nice. It is time to enter the role of personnel officer, hiring and firing.

One of the things I discovered at this stage is that a small business is like a jealous lover; it doesn't like to be left alone for too long. It's fully convinced it needs you and only you for its survival. You might try to palm it off on a surrogate, to slip in an office-manager unnoticed, but pretty soon it will start to squawk. Only you understand its peculiar idiosyncrasies. Only you can smooth the waters of the inevitable storms. Or so it seems. Understanding this is a good starting point to begin to pry off one or two fingers of its vice-like grip. Without additional staff the business stagnates and bringing new players into the game can provide an injection of fresh ideas. It can also be fraught with new challenges that will test all of your newly-acquired resources and people skills, as well as your trust in the Zen Factor, as the following example shows.

Screening the players

Matthew was hired to become office- manager. He was an affable sort of a young man, keen as mustard and highly ambitious - just the kind you could train up to take over the reins some day. He never walked anywhere; he ran, and almost clicked his heels to attention when you spoke to him. His voice was high-pitched and a little strained, with a slightly effeminate turn of phrase. He devoured the work in big chunks, priding himself on his efficiency. His energy was right up there. At times he seemed quite driven, as if chased by a hundred demons or as if he had to constantly prove his worth. Either way, he came with an impressive dossier and seemed ideal for the job.

One thing that the recruiting agency had failed to discern at the interview was that he smoked heavily. Any enquiry into this subject was regarded as being discriminatory and therefore not allowable to be asked, regardless of any potential mismatch with the ethos of the workplace that they placed him in. Several times a day, Matthew would dash outside to gulp down a few furtive inhalations before returning in a cloud of smoke to his desk, filling the air with the distinctive smell and leaving traces all over the computer and phones. It was obvious that smoking simply didn't fit in with the ethics and values of this particular business.

When he mentioned he wanted to give up the habit I offered to help if I could. That was on Friday. On Monday morning he was in the office unusually early and clearly agitated. He said he hadn't slept all weekend, such was his rage. He had prepared several pages of notes which he read out in a shaky voice. The gist of it was that he felt he was being discriminated against and he shouldn't have to quit smoking to keep the job. I agreed with him. Despite this, he went on to hand in his resignation as of immediately, demanding four weeks' pay in lieu and threatening to take me to the equal-opportunities tribunal if I objected. I wasn't objecting. I could see that he was in a double-bind, a part of him wanting to quit smoking and stay, another part totally resistant to such an idea. Clearly that side had won.

Connection in conflict

In such a situation there are two possible ways of responding; one is to be swamped by negative energy and give back more of the same, becoming embroiled in a 'who's right and who's wrong' type of argument. Or it is possible to view the other person sympathetically, appreciating their predicament whilst maintaining one's own peace. We still can connect with others, despite apparently being at odds. I find that the best way to do this is to centre myself using the previously-mentioned technique of sensing some part of my body, usually my hands. Sensing the body from the inside like this is the quickest way of coming back to a more centered place of stillness. It seems to help defuse melodrama and to calm people down. The higher vibration of peace overrides the lower vibration of distress, just as light replaces darkness.

The one who has the most choices available to them is the one who has inner freedom. This is the freedom that extends far beyond any physical boundaries that might be imposed on us. It is an inner freedom that cannot be bought or sold as it is priceless. On that Monday morning, after sitting through the discomfort, things started to quieten down at last. We agreed things weren't working for both of us and it would be best for him to go. He requested a positive written reference which I provided, wishing him every success in any future position he might hold. For me, it was over, already moved into the past. I hoped it was the same for Matthew.

We can learn that even in the midst of turmoil it is possible to maintain one's inner peace. It takes practice as well as cultivating a certain mind-set. This comes back to our self-talk, the voice that speaks from the ego or from a higher source. Each is recognizable by its fruits: one bears distress, anger, and separatism; the other, peace, compassion and harmony. It is never worth trading one's peace for anything, no matter how serious it may seem at the time. Ask yourself how it will seem a year from now, or five or ten years, or even a hundred? Will you even remember it?

Not long after Matthew's departure he was replaced by a delightful woman, Carrie, who was referred by a friend of a friend in the magical ways of happenstance and synchronicity. Carrie was to become the lynch-pin in holding things together in the office, as well as a cheery face to greet each morning. She was quick to learn the business and was very well organized. When any part of stock levels dropped she was onto it. We had been caught out before with not having all the parts on hand for the next production run. Sometimes lead-times doubled or suppliers ran out of critical components. All rather frustrating, especially if a major advertising campaign was pre-booked. Can you imagine your own reaction at such times? Which way would you jump? To anger, blame and despair, or to acceptance and moving on regardless. I certainly don't claim to always have opted for the latter. Occasionally things got the better of me and I allowed myself to be adversely affected. However, despite these obstacles the business was growing rapidly, moving forward with a determination and certainty of direction, like a horse that knows its way home.

Peanuts for monkeys

It is one thing to feel peaceful, calm and in control of oneself whilst only being on our own or with a close friend. Throw in a few extra characters, of diverse types and we are often tested. Being tested is a good thing; it provides more opportunities for what Gurdjieff called 'the Work', meaning the inner work on ourselves. It is all well and good to sit and meditate quietly in a cave and feel one is progressing quite well. Only after leaving the cave and interacting with others in the outside world can we ascertain our true level of development. And more often than not, it is not as pretty as we'd like to think. But therein lies its value to us. We now have some external indices, some checks and measures, to provide us with some feedback.

The following example shows how important it is to remain connected to your own vision and inner guidance. As my business grew, more resources were available for extra staff, preferably experienced and affordable - two often incompatible requirements. Compromises must be made, sliding the scale on each of these preferences slightly away from the centre until they find a happy match.

After having written the new job description I began interviewing for a "Sales and Marketing Coordinator". I used the word "Coordinator" because the title "Manager" implied a higher salary. We were not yet able to offer much, but the potential was there for performance to be rewarded. I worked out a base salary plus bonuses and commissions that depended on achieving certain sales targets. We received about a dozen applicants, most completely unsuitable.

Then in walks Paul with fifteen years' experience in our industry and a proven track-record in sales. He wows Carrie and me with his dossier of achievements. In fact, after an hour and a half, he has us completely mesmerized. We need no further convincing; the position seems tailor-made for him. Never mind that he is saying that just about everything we have done up to now is off-track and will need re-designing. He is the man to do it. He can give us a whole new look with uniformity. We have to agree there; we have evolved in rather a hotchpotch way. He is the new broom who can sweep up our mess, get rid of those distributors who are not a hundred percent behind us; weed out the sales-reps with a ho-hum attitude. He is promising the earth and our tongues are hanging out. We can almost taste the abundance he offers. Yes, yes, yes!

And then he sets us straight on what it is we really need. Not a full-time person sitting all day at this brand new work-station, wasting our precious resources with an inefficient use of time. What we really need is a 'Consultant', someone who only gets paid for the hours he works. Surprisingly, we are still nodding along, despite this radical departure from what we originally thought we needed. Paul assures us that he can accomplish in a few hours what might take others a week. He reminds us that the pitifully low salary we are offering will only attract new graduates, and remember, "If you pay peanuts, you get monkeys."

So now it just comes down to price. How much is it going to cost us to secure the valuable services of this expert?

"Well of course I won't charge you what I would normally charge," Paul calms us. "I haven't come here to rape and pillage."

After a few more minutes of negotiating, we settle on half his normal hourly rate. He leaves, asking me to call him when I have worked out how many of his hours we can afford. There is an almost feverish air left in his wake, in which I attack the books, juggle and tweak the budget to see how much strain it can take. It's reasonably healthy so can stand a fair bit. I call and let him know we can manage to hire him for three days a week. He says he will think about it and let me know. About an hour later, he calls back and announces jovially that it's a done deal; he will start on Monday. Carrie and I are jubilant, as if having just won the lottery.

I go back to my desk and write up a new employment contract, removing all the sales' targets, bonuses and commissions and then factor this new expense into the budget. It grates a little, but I remind myself that "you have to break an egg to make an omelet" and the investment will certainly pay off. After all, this man has turned a failing restaurant into a booming success, reaping 1.8 million dollars per annum consistently for over ten years.

Briefly I question why he is still seeking employment, given his hugely successful past? Less briefly, I begin to have some qualms and feel uneasy in the pit of my stomach. I start to feel like someone coming out of a magic spell or as if some mind-altering drug is wearing off. Griping little pangs of doubt begin to gnaw at me. I start to get that niggling little sense of having in some way been duped. My inner voice is squawking and I have to listen to it.

I ask myself, what have I done? I answer: I have gone shopping for a VW and been shown a brand new Porsche – infinitely more appealing, but way out of budget. And that small part of me that likes to dream big and override all reason says, "Why not?" Every entrepreneur likes to take risks and I am no different. But when I reflect on some of the earlier risks I have taken, they were all much more carefully calculated - not done on an impulse the way some people go on spending sprees for 'retail therapy'. When I rang Paul to graciously decline his wonderful offer, he was good-natured about it, laughingly adding "that was the shortest job I never had".

A few weeks later I hired Melanie, our new-graduate in Sales and Marketing, to sit all day, all week at her new work-station. She fitted into our little group quite well, bringing her lunch-box full of home-made vegetarian delights to share at lunchtime. She also brought a plethora of a fresh graduate's new ideas and enthusiasm with her. Her energy was good and it is energy that fuels growth. It might not be as flashy or as fast as a Porsche but at least we were moving in the right direction at our own pace.

Unlikely teachers

It is possible to come to value our so-called 'enemies' as our greatest teachers. It is relatively easy to feel relaxed and comfortable with those who agree with us and who share the same values. Amongst such people we are seldom challenged or made to look at ourselves more closely. They like us just the way we are, because we are pretty much like them. Whereas those whose views differ from ours often rub us the wrong way, testing our patience. We can argue the point, dismiss them as being simply 'wrong', or look more closely for the lesson. If projection is perception then what we are seeing in them is something that we recognize, something from within ourselves. And it is always something we don't want to see or something we don't like. We have the choice to heed the lesson or not. If we ignore it, it will reappear at some other time, perhaps in some other form and perhaps more violently. It demands our attention. We are here to grow. Every single thing provides an opportunity for that growth. Here is a realization from *"A Course in Miracles"* that is beneficial to meditate upon:

"I am responsible for what I see.
I choose the things I experience.
I decide the goal I would achieve.
Everything that seems to happen to me.
I ask for and receive as I have asked."

Chapter 9

The shape of dreams

Less than a year and a half after starting up the business, it was time to buy the big boat. The first stage of the dream was about to become reality! Although the budget was tight, it was obvious the cash flow was improving and could support a loan. I decided to stretch a little and enjoy the fruits of my labors concurrently with their growth. Also I was well aware of the fact that prior to casting off into the wild blue yonder, I would need at least another year of sailing experience. I have seen so many people hold back until they feel that absolutely everything is ready before they leap, and very often it never happens. They become the ones who are full of regrets later in life, wishing they had pursued their dreams more ardently at the time. In fact there is a very narrow window of opportunity for doing so, as is the case with many activities in life. Hence the old adage: "seize the day!"

It was time to sit and do some creative visualization, using all the tools at my disposal to conjure up the perfect boat for me. And of course to go out and do the leg-work, scouring the ads and visiting the brokers. For some people, this search can take years, as they go from boat to boat with their extensive checklist in hand. For me, it was much quicker, as the same wondrous synchronicity brought us together.

Meant to be for me

It was on the way back to the airport, that I felt compelled to make a last-minute stop at another brokerage. And there she was - sitting alongside the dock having just sailed in from San Francisco - without even a 'For Sale' sign up yet. The owners were on board, a youngish German couple, looking tanned, fit and strong from several months of cruising. They spotted me admiring their boat and invited me on board to have a look around. She was exactly as I had pictured in every last detail. Absolutely perfect!

Within minutes the broker arrived and sat himself squarely in the companionway in a position of control. After a short while he pulled out an Owner's Manual and began describing some of the boat's unique features and virtues. There were a great many, all of which were in accordance with my own notions of what should be. He could see I was interested and asked how much time I had to spare before needing to be at the airport for the flight home. I figured about one hour. At that point he did something that doesn't normally happen –

he asked the owners to take me out for a sail. This is most unusual. At very least there would be some discussion about price and some agreement to purchase if the test-sail was satisfactory. There was none of this. We simply cast off the dock-lines and headed out to sea.

The weather was putting on its best behavior, with a light nor' easterly breeze and a few cotton-wool clouds garnishing a clear blue sky - just the kind of day that makes everyone who doesn't have a boat want to own one. We hauled up the mainsail and then the large genoa, both in near-new condition with the cut and cloth of high-performance sails. Once the engine was cut, she was away, gliding along as effortlessly as a big white bird. That has always been a favorite moment for me, just then, in that second, when the thrumming vibration of the diesel gives way to silence and the wind takes over. As the sails billow and fill and the windward side of the hull lifts up as if it were weightless, the boat comes to life. With the plumb bow splitting the waves, tossing droplets of spray out either side, this is what she was made for; this is where she belongs.

I took the wheel and marveled at her responsiveness to the slightest touch, the barest finger-tip control. Never before had I experienced such a well-balanced, light helm on a keel-boat of this size. The smallest movement of the wheel to one side or the other and instantly she turned in that direction. A more rapid quarter turn of the wheel spun her into the tack, turning virtually on her own length. At that moment I had the biggest grin on my face as I knew with absolute certainty, this is my boat, this is it!

Only the price was a bit of a stumbling block; she was almost twice what I had allowed for. But by then the Germans and I had established a rapport, recognizing our common appreciation of the same things. They were delighted to have found someone who would love their boat as much as they did and agreed to reduce the price. It was still a lot more than my budget, but the broker completely ignored this fact as if it didn't matter in the least. He could arrange finance, he offered. How on earth he knew I could repay such a sizeable loan was quite beyond me, but the path seemed to be cleared with no objections left. It was one of those cases of "bite off more than you can chew and then chew like crazy". The means would come. I was confident of that.

Going for it

In the space of an hour we were back at the dock, the papers all signed. We were so overcome by emotion we were hugging each other like long-separated lovers. The broker and his wife were also visibly moved and commented it was nothing at all like their usual boat sales; it seemed more like handing over the Holy Chalice. This was clearly a special occasion; one in which the sense that something more than meets the eye is present. To me, it seemed as if everything else in my life had been leading up to that moment and there was no other way it could have been. I felt filled with an enormous sense of gratitude. At that point, I didn't fully understand exactly what it was I had bought or just how unique it was, but all that would become clear with time. She was a true thoroughbred. The Germans had cared for her with all the fastidiousness expected of their race and had spared nothing in fitting her out for a world circumnavigation. She had everything needed to go again with me at her helm and I could already envisage that thrill.

A few weeks later, a couple of friends and I sailed triumphantly into our home port to be met by a welcoming party brandishing champagne flutes and bottles of Moet and Chandon by the dozen. We fastened the dock-lines and felt that sigh of relief that comes at the end of a passage, when both crew and boat are tired but at the same time victorious. We had been through something together and shared in the challenge of overcoming the trials of the sea, as well as the honor of learning more of our valiant steed's capabilities. She had done it admirably and we all had an increased measure of respect for her breed. Everyone piled aboard and raised a toast to the newcomer. It was a fitting acknowledgement of what they all saw as a truly phenomenal achievement; there she was in all her salt-drenched glory, the testimony to dreams made real, well before anyone believed it could possibly be done.

Both ends of the stick

It is easy to feel elated when everything is going well. We can quite easily get caught up in the momentum of success, to the extent that we risk becoming bigheaded and egotistical. From there it is only a short step to becoming aloof and selfish, thinking more of ourselves than of others. We can begin to regard ourselves as being in some way special and superior, above the common rabble beneath us. Our own desires seem more important than others and like pampered children we expect to get our own way. It is not a mature perspective; rather it is one that engenders negativity and loss of respect, both in others as well as within ourselves.

Similarly, when we encounter losses or too many obstacles in our path we can feel vexed to the point of complete despondency. This is simply the other end of the same stick. We are still being buffeted by the winds of chance and seeing ourselves as at their mercy. Any contradictory word that ruffles our feathers, any situation that we don't like, any problem that we didn't anticipate, upsets our world. We can be thrown off balance by just about anything. Our equanimity is gone.

We can see instances of this see-saw ride happening even in the course of a single day: a morning phone call may herald a break-through acceptance by a major retail outlet; later on, a supplier might call to say they can no longer get the same caps we have been using on our jars. First we are jubilant; next we feel we can't go on. There seem to be so many factors outside of our own control that we are dependent on just to be able to keep the doors open. These can get into you like worms and cause many a sleepless night.

Identification

There is a relevant fable that serves as a reminder. The king of an ancient land summoned the wisest man in the kingdom to his palace. He asked the wise man to make him an object, just one thing, which would help maintain his equanimity; something that would sober his mood when he was overly excited and full of pride and that would raise his spirits when he was downcast. Later on the wise man returned. He handed the king a small box, within which was a simple gold ring. The inscription on the ring read: "This too will pass".

Remembering the transient nature of all things

can help us to be less identified with them. Whenever we lose ourselves so deeply within the vagaries of the external world, we open ourselves up to suffering. A man may drive an expensive sports car and live in a big house full of antiques and fine art treasures and think himself happy. Yet in many ways he is owned by these things, rather than owning them. If he identifies himself with them to such an extent that they are almost part of him, they define who he is in the world. Then these status-symbols of power and position define the man himself. Small wonder that so many cast themselves from windows of tall buildings when the stock market crashed. They couldn't face the thought of going back to the bottom rung of the ladder.

It is easy enough to get caught up in the excitement of owning a magnificent ocean-going yacht; sobering to remember all the additional responsibilities that it brings. Every single thing we own, in some way owns us. We are bound by our possessions and it is sometimes hard to remember how ephemeral and fleeting they are, just like our physical bodies. Even the body carries with it responsibilities to care for it, feed it, bathe it, clothe it, rest it, exercise it, and so on. Our homes are the same: places that need to be regularly cleaned and maintained. Every single one of our personal belongings requires some of our attention at some time. These things can almost become an extension of our selves and to lose them is akin to losing one's right arm. All of these considerations are more obviously present when a small business is accelerating fast and rich rewards are being reaped.

Buddhism advocates walking the middle path, and warns us it is attachment that is the main cause of all human suffering. It seems to be part of the human condition to become attached to things, to people, to ideologies, beliefs and opinions. This is the stuff that wars are made of. It is not always easy to remember that another person's opinion is just that – their opinion. A challenge to our own views seems to be an attack on ourselves. Why is that so? It certainly doesn't seem rational.

The driverless carriage

We are so strongly identified with our own thoughts that they seem to be woven into the fabric of our being. "I think; therefore I am", said Descartes. We rarely stop to consider where most of these self-defining thoughts have come from. Nature or nurture - genetic programming or environment and upbringing – either way, can we truly say they are our reality? Or is our 'reality', as we perceive it, simply a conglomeration of bits and pieces assembled from our past?

The Dalai Lama talks of special techniques

designed to cultivate the "awakening mind" - though he himself admits that he has not yet attained this state of omniscience. Even he is sometimes prey to the foibles and weaknesses of human nature which he strives each day to rise above. But he is on the path, moving towards it, practicing mindfulness and compassion for the sake of all other sentient beings. His Holiness has said that "We can achieve enlightenment only through the practice of meditation; without it there is no way we can transform our minds."

The mind is a wayward creature that often runs away with us, like a team of horses bolting before a driverless carriage. It is up to us to control the horses so they take us where we want to go. As His Holiness says, this can only be done through a regular meditation practice. Transformation of our world begins with transformation of our minds. Or, as I keep on saying: mastery of self precedes mastery of results.

How then, can we know if we are on the path to the desirable places – Nirvana, Heaven, omniscience, enlightenment - or not? Reason tells us that the only way to escape from misery is to recognize it, and then go the other way. When we are beset by even the tiniest doubts or fears, by even the faintest irritation or animosity, we can be sure we are heading away from the light and into darkness.

So the test is this: ask yourself how do you feel? What is your present energy like? Is it jangled and disconnected, or are you completely at peace within? Are you certain which way you are going? Is it toward the truth or away from it? This is a moment by moment assessment, not one that can be made on the basis of our past. It appears as if the past is a powerful entity that determines our present. Yet what has been, as well as what is yet to come, have all the influence that we ourselves have given them. And all our power to influence them in any shape or form is right here and right now.

Feedback

Only now, in this moment, are we able to actually do anything. Anything else is simply dreaming. We can dream of a time of peace yet to come, but if our present state is embroiled in tempest, the stage is set for more of the same. The acorn contains the oak tree. As mentioned earlier, one of my favorite sayings is that the definition of insanity is to keep on doing the same thing and expect to get different results. If what we have been doing up to now has not brought peace and happiness, why continue on in the same vein? To do so, and expect something different must make us wonder if we are in our right minds. Our life is a reflection of the choices we make in this present moment. We can choose heaven or hell. Some of the choices leading to misery are so well concealed it takes a fair degree of vigilance to spot them.

At the end of each day it is helpful to do a brief meditation and review of the day. "How did it all go? Was it in accordance with my goals? How do I feel about it? Is there a sense of uneasiness or of peace?" These questions pertain more to our inner world, from which important messages can be revealed with a gentle (or not so gentle) nudge of conscience. Our energetic state is a reliable indicator of whether or not we are operating in accordance with our higher selves.

It can also be beneficial to sit down quietly with pen and paper and make note of any practical suggestions for improvement. This exercise reviews our outer world and helps us to see how it is a reflection of the inner. Then the questions include things like "What could be done differently? Is anything else needed? What's missing? Have I overlooked anything important? How is everyone going? Have we had fun today?"

This is not a time for recrimination or self-deprecation. If mistakes have been made, see them as just that – mistakes. Errors require only correction, not judgment. It helps to remember that it really is impossible for us to judge anything at all. There are so many factors at play. How can we begin to piece together any kind of understanding of the whole from the few bits of information that our limited perception sees? It is like three blind men trying to describe an elephant from the small part of it that each can touch. One has the trunk, another feels the tail, the other touches a leg. To each of them it is quite a different beast, one part not connected to the other. When we lose our sense of interconnectedness, we can have no idea of the reality of an elephant or anything else.

The famous Zen master, Tozan, said, "The blue mountain is the father of the white cloud; the white cloud is the son of the blue mountain. They depend on each other, without being dependent on each other. The white cloud is always the white cloud and should not be bothered by the blue mountain. When we become truly ourselves, we are purely independent of, and at the same time, dependent upon everything."

If we lose our appreciation of this interdependency of everything, we are more easily bothered by things that appear to be outside of ourselves. Consider, for example, the absurd notion of a mutinous hand, (like Dr Strangelove's) that, having lost its identity, keeps on trying to strangle the body it is attached to. This example has pushed the concept out to the extreme for the sake of humor, but it still has validity. If we can remember that nothing exists independently in itself, it is easier to stay calm.

So even though we are dependent on things, like the food we eat, we are also independent. Only in the deep stillness within can we begin to understand this seeming paradox. But it is in this understanding that true freedom lies. This is perhaps easier to recognize in the way we can more easily forgive the transgressions of our own children, because they are part of us. The concept of forgiveness only has meaning in a divided world, a world of us and them. This is the central theme of "*A Course in Miracles*".

"Salvation is a paradox indeed. It asks you to forgive all things that no-one ever did; to overlook what is not there, and not to look upon the unreal as reality."

Chapter 10

Keeping on track

It may seem strange to be discussing ideas such as forgiveness, reality, separatism and unification in a book about business development. But when we remember that our business is in our lives and not vice-versa, we can appreciate the need for integration of all the various aspects of life, especially those that link us to a benevolent higher power. The essence of this force is love, which is perhaps an even stranger idea to introduce in this context. By now it should be becoming clear that love is in fact pre-requisite to every successful human endeavor. In chapter 2, I spoke of the importance of retaining the passion of the craftsman, the inner you who is in love with what you do, who strives to always do it to the best of your ability, and noted that this is the heart of the business. Let us now consider love in this light.

There are four faces of love: intention, attention, action and expansion. Love begins as an intention, or a desire for something or someone. Our will is involved when we will to become involved. There is a deliberate choice in which we do not see our own interests as separate from another's. Creativity enters at this point, since, as Dr Wayne Dyer has observed, "intention in itself is a force which aligns us with the all-creating universal mind".

Next comes the giving of our attention, to a greater or lesser degree, according to our capacity to give it. If we can focus our attention fully on the object of our desire, be it our business or our beloved, there is an intense experience of being connected. We give of ourselves, both in time and energy. In the same way as with our children, we lovingly nurture their growth and provide for all of their needs. Love is as love does. This is the action part, where we choose to act in loving ways for the betterment of another. When we strive for the growth of another we expand both ourselves and them. This expansion is the fourth facet of love through which notions of separation and judgment are relinquished.

Who's to blame?

In business, as in life, our first response to trouble is immediately to judge harshly, sometimes chiding ourselves, but more often than not, criticizing others. Set-backs can seem overwhelming but it is important to remember that it is what it is. No-one is to blame, because no-one deliberately set out to sabotage things. Quite simply, it is what it is. If you go looking for reasons beyond this, it is a sure way to destroy peace. Mistakes happen and while checks and measures can go a certain way to counteracting these, at the end of the day they must be seen as simply mistakes. Any further judgment serves only to upset ourselves. In blaming or judging harshly, which is to say, with narrow-minded tunnel-vision that fails to take everything into account, we are the ones whose cages are rattled.

Stop a few moments to consider this more deeply. The common scenario following a mishap is to protest our own innocence; e.g. "I am certain I ordered the right sized bottles."

The next thing is to blame someone else: "They messed up and sent the wrong ones."

Then to judge: "They are incompetent fools. How could they do such a thing? Why is it that they always mess up?" etcetera, etcetera.

But now ask yourself, what is the effect of this way of thinking? Does it have any effect on them, the incompetent fools? Does it help them to be less incompetent in future? Does it guarantee they won't make the same mistake again? Granted, a part of us will be thinking, "yes, if I come down on them heavily enough, they might learn not to do it again, or at least, not to me" - just as a small child might be frightened by an angry parent into never doing whatever it was that displeased mum or dad ever again. But in the world of grown-ups, the irate customer is more likely to be dismissed as being irrational, belligerent, annoying and unpleasant to deal with. And meanwhile, ulcers are not growing in the imagined 'offender's' stomach, but in the blustering would-be dictator's. Of course, you will say, that is only logical, because they are not the ones suffering the consequences of their blunders. However, the fact remains that we can choose how to respond to things, to either increase, or ease our own suffering.

In these instances we can use any or several of the Zen Factor tools at our disposal. Sitting quietly following the breath will help to calm and restore our equilibrium, or we can try a more active form of meditation. For example, by observing where we feel the irritation in our body, we can then let it go or dissolve it, using whatever imagery works for us. Alternatively, knowing that memory and imagination share the same neural pathways, we can briefly recollect the whole string of events as it happened, then rearrange things to be the way we would prefer them to be. This new scenario needs to be vividly constructed, using all the senses, with vibrantly colorful sights, resonant sounds, profound tastes, smells and sensitive touch. The mind will then accept this new 'memory' in place of the old, and will clear the way for the improved scenario to be the way it was, is and will be. Having a more pro-active stance available at very least engenders a sense of empowerment.

The Moon or Mars?

A small business is rarely static; it is either in decline or in growth. All the written objectives of its development are based on growth. But it is important to find the balance between growth at any cost and human values of loyalty, kindness and decency. An empire based on blind greed will be weak at its core and eventually crumble. It is not too hard to recognize when we are off track. Just as when we are operating in accord with our higher selves everything flows smoothly, so too the opposite is true. It pays to be able to recognize the difference before it goes too far awry. The business plan will contain useful checks and measures, but an over-riding awareness of the spirit of the enterprise is needed. This is more of a gut feeling, a tuning in and checking if it feels right to you, in the same way that a parent knows when their child is out of sorts. Don't be fooled by the usual bumps in the road; check for dead-ends.

It's evident that being in business is often about things not going right. Mistakes get made; things get overlooked and pop up later to bite us. The decision-making process can lead down a blind-alley or onto a completely foreign road. At those times, it is as though we started off heading for the Moon and have somehow gotten side-tracked and find ourselves approaching Mars. At first sight, it seems as if we are still headed where we first intended. The similarity of the way fools us into believing the destination is the same. But we are off track and worst of all, without even knowing it. There may be other influences that have invisibly swayed us, in the same way as the gravitational fields of other planets. Other people have entered the sphere, bringing their own ideas of how things should be done. There are many more balls to juggle than before.

Look, no hands!

In the small-business's first year, everything had to be done by the book because there was no other way known. Come the successful passing of that first hurdle and suddenly there is another way other than the way we've just been. Why not a re-run of the first twelve months? We may think that has held us in pretty good stead thus far and ask ourselves why not just keep on keeping on? Sounds reasonable.

But a business in its second year is as different as a newborn baby to a toddler. Now we're walking mama. Look, no hands! We're up and away. Look out world! But the pitfalls now are bigger. We're no longer so lovingly nurtured and protected. We've made some gains and now have more to lose. There are holes in our bucket (many unseen) that need to be plugged or all that water will very quickly drain out.

New products are relatively easy to sell, especially if there's a need and a feel-good story to tell. Once it's been told it gets harder. Then things like how good the distributors' sales reps are matter more. It is their job to make sure the retailers don't forget about us. If they slack off we are left in a situation of having a great menu but lousy waiters. The customers will drift away. It is a team effort and everyone in the team has to be pulling in the same direction. The greatest energy is always expended at take-off. Once at cruising altitude that thrust can throttle back to such a degree there is a risk of stalling. All the players may not even be in the same game anymore.

Attracting the right people

Another example from my own business provides testimony to using the Zen Factor tools to work around obstacles and attract what is needed. There are some brilliant graphic designers out there and some not so good. The challenge was how to find the good ones to design some new marketing materials. There was too much at stake to simply concede to something that struck me as second-rate. It had to have an element of 'wow-factor', something distinctive that would make me sit up and take notice. While the old saying has it that you can't judge a book by its cover, the initial impact of something eye-catching may be sufficient to pick it up and at least read the blurb. After that, the item needs to speak for itself, but it is important initially to capture that attention.

Meanwhile, I was spending a lot of money on nothing and getting nowhere. I had to consider that perhaps another marketing company, or even some freelancing individual outside of the system, could do better. But how to find them? That question was answered for me in the way I trusted most, by giving it to my higher self in meditation. It is true that all things are solved in silence, by sitting quietly and turning within. The solution may not be immediately apparent but it will become so in due course. Often we have to abandon the pursuit, to stop pushing and let the answer find us. So I set the intention in an Outcome Meditation and waited.

A short time later, I was standing in a crowded room during a coffee break in a business conference on export markets. As I poured myself a cup of tea, I commented to the friend who had accompanied me, "What I really need right now is a brilliant graphic designer." Eavesdropping on this comment, the man standing behind me handed me the business card of someone who had done some work for him. My first thought was, "oh no, not another blind alley" but I decided to take a chance on this one, given the unusual circumstances of the introduction. So I made the call and within the week, was sitting opposite a most unlikely looking, red-headed youth.

What most impressed me about this young man was the way he listened. You could almost see his intelligence at work as he sat in our office taking notes. His efficiency was quite startling. Not only had he come to our pre-arranged meeting on time, but in less than an hour of listening intently to the brief, he was obviously tuned in to the requirements of the task. It was as if we were of one mind - only his was able to take it that step further to materialization.

And so, after weeks and weeks of chasing our own tails, there it was, a work of art that all of us instantly recognized as perfect. Not one of us stood back to withhold judgment for a moment. No-one prevaricated, "um"-ed or "ah"-ed or showed any reserve. We simply shook our heads, laughed in disbelief and knew beyond a shadow of a doubt that this was what we had been looking for. It was quite amazing, miraculous, and unbelievable - that is, if you didn't appreciate the power of the Zen Factor. Regardless, evidence of the universe providing us with the things we ask for, never ceases to instill in me a great sense of awe, reverence and gratitude.

Giving thanks

Gratitude is an important part of creating a life that is open to receiving. Otherwise the ego can rush in to claim credit which is like a wave claiming to be the ocean. Certainly the wave is a part of the ocean and can partake in the full power of that unified force, but alone it is nothing. The wave cannot create the ocean, just as we alone cannot create reality. It is only in joining that everything becomes possible. Tapping into the power of the ocean is not done with arrogance or pride, but humility and gratitude. It is vitally important to acknowledge this by stopping to give thanks. I cannot make this point strongly enough.

For those of you with a faith in a Deity, such as God or Allah, or any of the other names of a Divine Creator, call upon this name and give thanks. For others, use whichever term resonates, such as Spirit, Light, Love, Universal Intelligence, etc. All of these names are but names and as such are inherently inaccurate and limited. It is the energy that is behind the words that points to a possibility that in-spires us, which is to say, fills us with spirit, inspiration, love and gratitude. The energy of that higher vibration can only be experienced through raising our own vibrations beyond the physical realm. The way to do this is in the silence of deep contemplation and meditation. So when gifts come your way, be sure to reciprocate in kind.

Giving back in kind is an interesting thing to consider. Well you might ask, how can we possibly give back anything that comes anywhere close to the gifts we have received from the Almighty, the Creator of all, the Unknowable, the Source of everything? The answer is, in exactly the same way! That is, by matching the vibrational frequency of the benefactor and the spirit in which those gifts came, in other words, giving of ourselves. It is an indisputable truth that we get back what we give. To get love, give love; to gain respect, give respect.

Whenever we come from a place of fear or lack, this becomes a mirror reflecting the same back to us. Ask and ye shall receive. It cannot be otherwise. If our thoughts are full of doubts, we live in doubt. That is the world we inhabit and the world we inhibit. Ask yourself what kind of a world do you want to be in? A sad one, that sees suffering everywhere, where nothing goes right for you, or a happy world, where everything you need is available, exactly at the right time, in exactly the right form.

20:20 Hindsight

There is an old Greek saying that roughly

translated means "my later wisdom, if only I had you now". We all wish we were blessed with 20:20 hindsight to spot pitfalls in advance, but mostly it is only when we look back on things that the 'could-haves' and 'should-haves' become apparent. But life is for learning and we learn best from our mistakes, not from self-recrimination over what we should have done. We did our best at the time with the resources, information and prescience available to us. If the path was completely smooth and easy, we might never be tested and never come to know our strengths. Without the struggle to emerge from the chrysalis, the butterfly will never fly. So too, we bat our folded wings against the sharp edges of life to learn that the obstacles, like our so-called enemies are our greatest teachers. An 'obstacle' might simply be the result of a wrong turn. An 'enemy' need not be operating from malice or with the intention of causing harm; it can be enough for them to present an opposing view. Sometimes a persuasive argument can pull you off track, especially if that track is relatively new and not well known.

In a fledgling business, it is easy to fall under the spell of fast-talking salesmen who make you think that they know better than you. Especially once a degree of success has loosened up the purse-strings, and the budget for things like marketing is much bigger. There is more available to spend and as always, you want to spend it wisely, gaining maximum results for minimum expenditure. Where to allocate these funds is the big question. There will always be an abundance of experts who flock in to fill the void with what can be hard-sell advice. You need to be able to cut through the hype to recognize if what they are offering is consistent with your goals and in keeping with the company image. Often they will make totally outlandish proposals based on companies with much bigger budgets or with products that already have existing brand awareness.

Subtle obscurity

Here is an example of how easy it is to succumb to believing in the promise of fashionable campaigns. The fashion of the moment was for subtlety bordering on minimalist obscurity. This produces the kind of advertisement that people look at quizzically, wondering what it is trying to say, and even wondering what it is an ad for. Such ads are usually found in print media, such as in magazines and on billboards, where the viewer has the possibility of reflecting for a longer period of time, indeed, much longer than the brief moments allowed by fleeting images on a TV screen. The idea behind it is to get people's attention and make them stop and think, rather than spelling it all out for them. It can be very effective in capturing people's interest, leading them in with subtlety rather than a hammer. I have often found myself puzzling over a huge billboard with mostly empty space and some tiny cryptic message.

It can be rather satisfying to reach that "ah-ha!" kind of a moment when the penny drops and you get it. It makes you feel almost complicit in the whole marketing strategy, as if they have somehow pulled you into their world; inside from out in the cold. You are now not just inside but on-side, where you feel warm and welcome, part of the family. This works well if the product in question is already well established in the market place, but can fall flat on its face otherwise.

We didn't have the benefit of this hindsight at the time of being sold our first big-budget marketing campaign. That day, we were feeling quite important and serious, like five year-olds about to begin school. We had come of age and were ready to play with the big boys. Two very slick salesmen sat in our office for several hours, explaining the concepts and showing us A3 cardboard mock-ups of a series of graphics for full-page, full-color magazine advertisements. At first we didn't get it at all, but as time went on, their enthusiasm began to rub off on us and we grew similarly excited. In the heat of the moment we signed up for the full campaign.

The normal method of gauging the efficacy of

our advertising was first and foremost the internet. We could monitor exactly how many 'hits' we received on the website as well as how many enquiries and how many mail-orders came in. It was not a particularly large representation, but gave a fairly accurate precursor of what to expect at store-level. On this occasion however, following the publication of a very obscure full-page ad in a major magazine, there was nothing. Zip. Not even the tiniest little blip on the radar. The outside world had disappeared, or might as well have. More accurately, we had disappeared.

We took these results (or rather lack of results) back to the marketing gurus. They argued it was early days, that it was necessary to run the whole campaign to see the full effect. I argued I didn't have the budget for that kind of experimentation. It could cripple us. In hindsight I saw that it had taken two highly convincing men several hours to explain the concepts of the campaign to us; the general public didn't have that extra information available to them. They only had the stand-alone advertisement to go by. And most people, it seemed, were just not getting it. It was all just a little bit too obscure. People were not prepared to put in the time or effort to work it out. Even my own father failed to find the full-page ad, despite knowing it was somewhere in the magazine I had given him. When I directed him to it, he just shook his head in bewilderment. Sometimes, he advised, the obvious needs to be stated. It was yet another lesson in the continuous learning curve of being in business.

Blinking

The Zen Factor works when we tap into our higher self and listen to our inner voice, or 'gut feeling'. Most often it is our very first reaction to things that is the tell-tale sign as to what we really feel about it. There may be a slight flutter like 'butterflies' in the stomach; there may be some other physical sense, such as smell or taste. But contained in that gentle nudge is always a knowing. This concept has been explored in depth in Malcolm Gladwell's brilliant book *"Blink"*.

Usually we don't consciously know how we know something; we simply do. It happens in the blink of an eye. There is only a split second in which we are aware of 'something' that is trying to communicate with us. That something is, in part, testimony to the incredible power of the human mind, which is capable of processing millions of bits of information instantly, many of which are beyond conscious awareness. We constantly gather facts from everyone and everything we come into contact with, most of which are considered irrelevant and discarded, or stored away in the backs of our minds.

But more than this, there is additional information available to us which we recognize as in some way coming from beyond us. We have all had the experience of somehow knowing something that we know we did not know. It has a different quality, a sense of wonderment about it that begs the question, *"Where did that come from?"* This is the knowing that comes from connecting with a much vaster realm of consciousness, the unified mind of Zen. In this state of raised awareness, much more information is available to us that is far beyond our own limited perspective. It places us more firmly in the Now, expanding time and allowing us to awaken more fully to the present moment. Only in the present moment can this knowing be realized.

It takes time to develop trust and confidence in this gift. It also requires an inner stillness for the small, quiet voice to be heard above the raucous chatter that normally fills our minds. How can we listen when we are so noisy? How can we be still when we are so busy? Our cultural heritage is to ignore or override such feelings. They are deemed irrational because they cannot be understood or explained. We are reluctant to voice our doubts or to stand up to others who seem to know more than we do. We go along with things even when we know we shouldn't. It takes a lot to stand apart and question if this is the right way for us. But through the practice of stillness, more space is created for truth to guide the way. If you have a problem, ask what the lesson to be learnt from it is, take it in, learn from it, and move on.

Chapter 11

Interpretations

There are not too many people who can enjoy the fruits of their labors concomitantly with their growth. It is a choice - one that I personally preferred and saw the value of in many respects. So Wednesday afternoons became rather sacrosanct and I took a few hours off to go racing. That mid-week break out on the water provided a refreshing respite; it blew away the cobwebs and recharged my energy in a way that only a completely different activity from the daily routine can do. Plus it fitted in with my ultimate goals in a tangible and reaffirming way. If I was eventually going to sail across oceans I needed to prepare for it, with practical sailing experience and theoretical studies in navigation and seamanship.

I had a regular crew of four or five who were dedicated starters each week and it was an enjoyable social event with a few drinks up in the club after. There were other benefits to the business through those connections too. Many members of the yacht club were successful business people who were also able to draw a line through their diaries to go sailing mid-week. They were their own bosses. The post-race conversations in the members' bar were not only about race tactics but business dealings as well. A lot of information sharing went on in a very informal way and I always paid close attention. It pays to work your network and very often this is found in so-called 'leisure' time.

I always enjoyed this type of investigation, following up on the slightest leads and back-tracking out of dead-ends, always with the assurance of being guided by the Zen Factor. To deny this gift is only due to the self-aggrandizement of the ego which mistakenly believes itself to be in charge. Yet it makes no sense at all to expect our 'small self', with its limited perspective, to be able to know the whole. Only our 'higher self', beginning from a place of emptiness or no-mind, can be open to receive guidance. The cup of the ego is far too full for that. Others' stories are usually interesting and inspiring, creating a sense of "possible in the world, possible for me." Inspiration is the fuel that feeds our own fires.

Eighth sense

Nothing new can come into your life until you are grateful for everything already in your life. It is easy to overlook smaller miracles, focusing only on major events. But it is the minutia of our day-to-day lives that contain a wealth far beyond recognition and provide us with the greatest opportunity to grow. By paying closer attention to the present moment we come closer to the truth. This is never more evident than in our dealings with others, who hold up a mirror to ourselves.

It is easy enough to stay centered and calm when on one's own but as soon as we start to interact with others that equanimity is tested. It is then that who we are is revealed, both to ourselves and to the world. "I can't hear what you are saying over the screech of who you are," is a typical expression of the ambiguity we sometimes present.

How does this information transmit? Why is communication so much more than words? The fact is we only use a tiny fraction of our brain's capacity and ignore the vast resource beyond that. When information arrives from someplace other than the common five senses, we attribute it to something less tangible such as 'intuition' or a sixth sense - never considering the seventh, eighth and beyond.

An interesting experience of mine occurred in a public swimming pool where I used to swim a few laps early in the morning. Usually I had the place to myself, which meant I didn't have to worry about bumping into anyone else in my lane. I swam with my head mostly submerged, wearing earplugs, goggles and bathing cap. On this particular morning, another person entered the pool without me seeing them do so. Somehow, I was aware of their presence before I saw them swim by me in the next lane. This had me puzzled for a moment, before I realized I could 'smell' them.

Over the subsequent weeks I found that everyone had a slightly different smell and I began to recognize them in advance as their familiar scent was transmitted underwater. Since my nose was submerged at the time and not inhaling air, (the usual medium that carries scent), it was hard to explain. It made me wonder if this was something akin to the sense other underwater mammals or fish use to sense things far beyond their range of sight.

There is a recognized phenomenon known as 'synaesthesia' where different senses merge, such as colors with sounds, so a person might 'see' the note E-minor as blue. Obviously this refers to an inner kind of seeing, something 'seen' other than with the physical eyes. Throughout the ages, there have been many references to the visions of 'seers', who have accessed information via channels other than the physical. Understanding this keeps us open to other ways of gathering information than the usual. Our gut feeling or intuition can become a more reliable source. We can listen more attentively to the still, small voice within.

Symbols of symbols

As we found earlier, in many of the occasions when we are conversing with someone, we are not really listening to them. First and foremost, this is because we struggle to give our undivided attention to another for any length of time. It takes a deliberate, conscious effort. On top of this is the rather unfortunate fact that many of us have already formed our own opinions about everything. This is a lifelong process that takes place from birth. As infants, we are vitally alert to our environment and have an enormous desire to learn. We are like human sponges, soaking up information as fast as we can. Our very survival depends upon it. We need to know what is safe and what is dangerous. The answers often bind us, narrowing our experience of the world and quashing our natural instincts to explore. We are taught not to talk to strangers, not to run too fast, not to laugh out loud in class.

Young children quickly come to the stage of asking "why?" of everything. These are the questions that most perplex parents. "Why are you doing that?" or more often, "Why can't I do this, or that?" with each logical answer followed immediately by another "Why?" And bit by bit, we fill in the gaps on our blank slate, until, upon reaching 'maturity', we are full. The questioning then slows down. We think we know it all. It becomes more of a matching process, to see if the answers fit with what we have already decided to be so. Thus we are closed off and are merely listening to our own opinions. No-one can tell us anything. This closed mind is very obvious to others who despair of reaching us or teaching us. Our cup is full of our own opinions, belief systems and ideas about everything. We can never really hear what anyone else has to say.

In business, clear communication is vitally important, especially when dealing with people from other cultures and backgrounds. When beginning to explore potential export markets, for example, with the Japanese, it helps to know something of their cultural expectations, if not also a few words of their language. But communication is not just about the words we speak; it is much more than this. Words are symbols of symbols and therefore twice removed from reality. The first symbol is our interpretation of what is; the second symbol is the language we use to describe it. Linguists since Noam Chomsky have long debated the connection between language, culture and cognition. Benjamin Lee Whorf was one of the first to discuss the theory of language shaping thought, while Edward Sapir, a founder of American linguistics, argued there is no external reality that we can know without the filter of language telling us what we are seeing and what it means.

An infant must first of all be introduced to an object, like, for example, a spoon, taught its meaning and function and then taught the word "spoon". After a few hundred repetitions, it is unlikely that the child will ever truly see the spoon again. The raw reality of what an object is in itself, its independent *'isness'*, will have been superseded by the symbols that provide its place in relation to other things. We live in a world of relativity and these symbols provide convenient means of communicating, so long as we remember their limitations.

The overflowing cup

To understand one another, we must be on the same wavelength in all respects. It is impossible for our minds to connect if we are full of ourselves. If we are puffed up with conceit or simply full of our own ideas about everything, then that is all we will hear. Whilst we might appear to be listening, our minds are often elsewhere. Our attention span is small and a lot of the time we are checking for correspondences in our own lives, seeing if it fits with what we already know. If it does, we can nod along comfortably; if it jars, we can dismiss it absent-mindedly. Much of this process is done absent-mindedly. This is not to say our listening is done empty-mindedly, which would be far preferable. An empty mind is a receptive mind. So we can begin, what is known in Buddhism, as 'emptying the cup'.

Even though it can help to contemplate emptiness intellectually, without direct experience it will remain simply a concept. It is necessary to go beyond concepts to come to a place where things are what they are, without judgment. Then there can be peace. This is not so easy to do and takes a good deal of practice. We have been led to believe that judgment is valuable and a sign of maturity. However, this can be a 'small-self' activity, bringing with it discontent, depression and confusion. This kind of judgment is used to categorize things into either good or bad, desirable or undesirable. It is based on preconceptions, group consensus, and arbitrary rulings about what is better or worse. It is based on perception, which as we have seen, is the result of our own projection. Hardly a reliable source.

Knee jerk reactions

Deep within all of us is a far more reliable source, one which you can be sure will lead to certainty and peace. You can develop trust in this through experience, testing it out in the small concerns of the present moment. But first it is necessary to have a willingness to let go of existing preconceptions. All that we think we know, all that we have absorbed since birth, all that has gone into making us who we think we are today; all of this must be relinquished. At first, this idea may disturb us and seem threatening to our very being as we understand it. But with a deeper understanding of our true nature, we realize there is no loss. Nothing valuable is being sacrificed.

The conglomeration of bits and pieces from the past that we cling to have served well to build a strong ego and it is this that feels threatened. Just like the 'watched pot that never boils', the ego too, doesn't like to be watched. It prefers the shadow of subterfuge and dark cloak of ignorance. It prefers us to be completely unaware of its workings, innocently proclaiming itself to be so much a part of us that it is in fact our self.

The belief that what we don't know can't hurt us does not apply. When we stumble about in darkness, as if wearing a blindfold, we are sure to bump into things. It is ignorance that keeps us bound, making knee-jerk responses to a two year-old's fears. Where is freedom then, when pressing button A always results in response B? How many repeat performances of the same story does it take before we learn the lesson? How long before we see the futility of attempting to do things the way we have habitually done them, regardless of the results? How long before we gladly let go?

Facts or fears

When I say that I entrusted the fulfillment of my objectives to the Zen Factor, it doesn't mean I sat back and did nothing myself. It means that I did all I could, took advantage of any assistance available to me, did my meditations, utilized other tools as appropriate - and then let it go. Beyond that point, there is no need to push the river. Having set the course the destination is assured, but there is no attachment to it. There is a confidence that it will manifest, but nothing to prove. The ego is not invited. It is more a case of taking the attitude, "it is what it is"; and "what will be, will be".

This may seem something of a contradiction, (as many paradoxes do) but it is quite possible to set our course and then confidently allow for its unfolding, without clinging to it as an absolute necessity that we depend upon. Anything we cling to as if it was an essential part of ourselves defines us as impoverished and needy and locks us into the world of suffering that the Buddha spoke of. Life is "dukkha" or suffering when we form attachments to impermanent things and identify ourselves with them.

It is possible to live our lives through conscious choice, choosing freedom rather than suffering. We can choose love instead of fear. When we choose a life that we love, the outer world (which is only a projection of our inner world) also falls into place. If we trust in this it helps maintain our equanimity, which is not to say we don't experience the normal human responses, such as sadness, anxiety or fear. We just see each of these feelings for what it is, without reading any particular interpretation into it. For example, we might feel downcast or upset and then interpret this as being because of something going on outside of ourselves.

There is nothing outside of ourselves that has the power to make us feel sad or weak or hopeless. Facts in themselves are quite neutral and can do no harm. If we strip away our interpretation of what happened, we are left with simply the fact itself. And this, no matter how harsh or traumatic it may appear, is what it is. The idea of trauma is something added after by us. It is our interpretation of the fact that causes the trouble. In the paradoxical way of Zen, we can glimpse this understanding that mind is the causative force in every instance of perceived difficulty, as all of our experiences are created and interpreted therein.

Shunryu Suzuki, reminds us in *"Zen Mind, Beginner's Mind"*: "Nothing comes from outside our mind. Usually we think of our mind as receiving impressions and experiences from outside, but that is not a true understanding of our mind. The true understanding is that the mind includes everything. When you think something comes from outside it means only that something appears in your mind. Nothing outside yourself can cause any trouble. You yourself make the waves in your mind. If you leave your mind as it is, it will become calm."

Different people will give different interpretations to things. How they see it is not something determined by the fact itself. It is always a reflection of what is within us. It is our own thoughts that are projected outward, weaving some fanciful tale, often to explain things in such a way as to make us appear the victim of circumstance. All of our interpretations of what is have come from the past. They have no reality in the present moment, other than what we give them. If we change our mind about this, the energy we have given them is dissipated and we are free to experience a deeper joy instead. To ask the question: "why fly with a sparrow's wings when we could soar with those of an eagle?" is to acknowledge that of ourselves, (that is, our small selves or ego/personality selves), we are limited.

Only the good fruit

There is a strong temptation to succumb to being overly critical, judgmental and wishing things were different than they are. This is particularly so when dealing with the demands of running your own business. Such thoughts are quite venomous to us and to everyone around us. This is the kind of resistance that separates us from each other and blocks access to the Zen Factor. It is criticism that destroys love. There is an old Sufi saying about this: to take only the good fruit that is offered from the master's hand and to spurn the bad, is to lack the humility that enables us to receive according to our needs. When we become so fussy as to choose only that which we consider good, rejecting all else, we place ourselves above our master. Our thinking becomes divisive and we suffer the consequences of making ill-founded decisions, based on our own limited perspective. Remembering our limitations helps us to adopt a more inclusive mind-set that is open to willingly and even lovingly accept what is, with gratitude. Healing can happen, on every level, physical, mental, spiritual and beyond.

On a higher level, there are no limits, anything we can conceive of is possible - but this also includes an attitude of humility and thankfulness. We are humbled in the awareness of a greater power, which is not of our making. We are grateful that this power is available to us to share. It is something that is not of us, but comes through us, so long as we stay out of the way and don't obstruct it. Humility and grace help in removing the blockages to the awareness of love's presence. As a clear 'conduit', seeming miracles can flow through us and our external reality becomes the manifestation of whatever we deem possible. We can be sure, that just as the present day technological advances were like science fiction to our forebears, so too, what is yet to be discovered might seem now.

Chapter 12

Other influences

The electro-magnetic field (EMF), 'aura' or 'etheric body', has been the subject of decades of research. It was popularized in the 1960's by the Russian, Seymon Kirlian, after whom the process of Kirlian photography is named. There has been a great deal of controversy around this since then. Evidence suggests that Kirlian photographs can show changes in the patterns, color and intensity of EMFs that somehow correspond to the physical and emotional status of those subjects being photographed. At the University of California Centre for Health Sciences, a leaf's EMF, or 'biofield' showed changes when approached by a human hand and pricked. Even when part of the leaf was cut off, the amputated portion still appeared on film. The EMF of the hands of a healer has been seen to merge with and influence that of her patient. Whether we accept this at face value or, as some have implied, as simply produced by 'water vapor', it does seem to tie in with a large number of empirical observations. I personally have seen and felt auras and have witnessed them change under the influence of my touch. To my way of thinking, effectiveness is a measure of truth.

If we can exert some influence beyond the confines of our physical bodies we begin to realize that we are not separate individuals. We start to appreciate that we have a part to play in the whole, and that we are responsible for our thoughts and deeds. If we can create our world, we can create the world that others come into contact with. The space and time we inhabit is but a small part of our broader existence. Why then, would we doubt that our thoughts can move mountains, that our dreams can become real.

Alpha-ing

Perhaps one of the simplest ways of influencing our world is through 'alpha-ing' things. This term has been coined from the level of brainwave activity named after the first letter of the Greek alphabet: 'Alpha'.

Brainwaves have been scientifically measured and divided into distinct levels, and although there is no universally accepted standard, the following table shows the mental activities associated with each range:

Name	Frequency	Associated with
Gamma	> 40 Hz	Problem solving; increased mental activity
Beta	13-40 Hz	Active concentration, anxiety or arousal
Alpha	7-13 Hz	Relaxation, pre-sleep/waking, twilight zone
Theta	4-7 Hz	REM sleep, dreaming, deep meditation
Delta	< 4 Hz	Deep sleep, no body awareness

As our brain waves slow down, we have fewer cycles per second of electrical impulses, (measured in Hertz) and thereby fewer thoughts. The alpha brainwave level is cultivated through regular meditation practice and brings many benefits. These include the following:

• A physically relaxed state, in which the body's automatic healing occurs

• A lucidity of mind and increased awareness

• More positive thinking; a natural anti-depressant

• An improved immune system

• Passive problem-solving ability; solutions present themselves

• The ability to tap into the Zen Factor and

higher levels of consciousness

- The ability to exert a positive influence over things

There is a specific technique that helps us to enter the alpha level more rapidly, which can be used anywhere, at any time. Being able to readily access this state provides us with all of the above benefits, but is mainly used when we wish to exert a positive influence in our world. This might be during a time of significant pressure, or simply when we need a car-park.

The groundwork for this is laid during our regular meditation practice. Firstly, we sit quietly; then take three longer and deeper cleansing breaths to begin slowing down. There are many different methods of entering a meditative state, and it is beyond the scope of this book to cover them all. The Buddhist meditation given in chapter 4, of following the breath, is sufficient for now. As our attention is centered on the incoming and outgoing breath our mental activity decreases, until we enter the deep relaxation associated with brainwave frequencies in the 7 – 13 Hz range. It is possible, but not necessary, to measure this.

The alpha level is then 'anchored' in the body, by holding the thumb and first two fingers together.

This is similar to the typically-portrayed posture of the meditating Buddha, although often only the Buddha's thumb and forefinger are shown to form a circle, with the other three fingers outstretched. Whichever posture feels comfortable for you will suffice, so long as it is the same one each time. Once this connection has become firmly established, the same posture will evoke the alpha state of slowed brainwaves and hence, closer proximity to the universal energy that empowers us. It is then possible to use this in our daily lives.

Practice alpha-ing small things at first, such as parking spaces, green traffic lights or lost keys. These are relatively easy to affect and will increase your confidence. Many is the time when I have needed a car-park and alpha-ed this wish prior to my arrival - then to find practically the whole street cleared of cars! Once when I was running so late for work that it was physically impossible to get there on time, I alpha-ed not only a straight run of green lights but time itself seemed to stop and I walked in a minute before my first client arrived. Theoretically, there is nothing that cannot be positively influenced in this way; it is a matter of accepting the possibility.

Grokking

In 1961, the author Robert Heinlein in his Sci-fi book *"Stranger in a Strange Land"* coined the term "Grokking" to refer to an interchange of intelligence that affects both observer and the observed. In his words:

"To grok means to understand so thoroughly that the observer becomes a part of the observed – to merge, blend, intermarry, lose identity in group experience. It means almost everything that we mean by religion, philosophy and science – and it means as little to us (because of our earthly assumptions) as color means to a blind man."

There are groups of modern-day 'Shamans' who practice grokking to influence tornadoes, hurricanes, earthquakes and volcanic eruptions, claiming success in averting or ameliorating many natural disasters – where such intervention is appropriate. If it isn't, or a better outcome will result from letting things take their course, then their grokking has no effect. As is the case in all these matters, the more minds that are joined with the same intent, the more powerful the influence.

The current dictionary meaning of grokking defines it as a state of rapport or empathy, i.e. "To share the same reality or line of thinking." This definition is more inclusive, acknowledging the interconnectedness of everything. In order to influence something, we must first become so deeply in touch with its essence as to practically become one with it; only then are we able to identify ourselves with its purpose, from which will follow the means to affect it in some way. From that place of unity, we are not 'influencing' in the sense of an outside force being applied to a separate object. When we are aligned with that object, it is as if we gain permission to 'drive the bus' for a while.

Which tool to use?

Grokking and alpha-ing are similar in this respect, both sharing an underlying principle of unification. There are of course many other methods of influence than these, (such as the use of symbols, tones, and color); and no doubt a great many more that we are as yet unaware of. In this domain, we are still very much in our early infancy. Notwithstanding, the tools we do have at our disposal are there for us to use, primarily to aid in our evolutionary development. The more we exercise our abilities, the stronger they become; and the more we contribute to recognizing ourselves as a more highly developed species.

The main difference between alpha-ing things and the Outcome Meditation is that the former is more immediately available and its results tend to be instantaneous. So we might tend to alpha up a break in the rain ten minutes before it is needed, whereas I used an Outcome Meditation to find suitable accommodation for one of my daughters, when rental properties were in short supply. The Alpha technique is very handy for finding appropriate solutions to problems of the moment; it provides a rapid entry into a more centered state when that is needed - (we might well ask, when isn't it?).

As with any of the other tools at our disposal, we often forget to use them, mainly because we are so heavily conditioned to believe that 'reality' comprises external events that happen to us. In Stephen Hawking's words: "What we regard as reality is conditioned by the theory to which we subscribe." If my theory is one of random chaos, I might regularly suffer the minor frustrations of mislaid documents, odd socks or lost keys. Rummaging through the 'black hole' of my carry-bag in search of the keys that I am sure are in there, it sometimes happens that I remember to alpha, then direct my hand to instantly find them. Sure enough, in the next second, they are found. It is that simple.

The Outcome Meditation is a more formal approach, requiring more time to set and usually a longer time-frame within which to happen. My declaration that "we have made an alliance with enthusiastic, well-qualified people, who are ready, willing and able to import and distribute our products throughout the UK, Europe and beyond" was soon to be realized. As with all Outcome

Meditations, I had put a date on this declaration, which is important for its manifestation within that timeframe. Again, it is best not to limit things by being too conservative, so I always add the proviso, "or sooner" to whichever date I have chosen. The choice of 'when' is not an arbitrary thing, but based on what seems achievable within that time, and then halved or quartered or divided by whatever amount the Zen Factor suggests. There is no point in being too reasonable when asking for things.

The double-headed arrow

When our new export partners arrived in my office, I was dressed in my corporate best and keeping sensation in both hands. The familiar tingling, pins and needles feeling kept me firmly grounded, centered within myself and awake to the present moment. My attention was like the double-headed arrow, going from my centre to theirs and back. For many people in situations like this, the focus is mainly on oneself, worrying about how I look, how I sound, what they are thinking of me. This creates feelings of nervousness, anxiety and stress; awkwardness pervades the atmosphere, making everyone feel just a little uncomfortable or ill at ease. Conversely, when awareness has a unified focus, one's self becomes a less important player in the game - despite the fact that the warmth, ease and welcome are being intentionally created. The trust that this is so is a gift that comes through us but is not of us. It is the Zen Factor at work.

It has never ceased to amaze me how this works. Time and again, I have witnessed the power of sensation linking minds together in an enveloping common bond. On that particular day, the space we shared was as precious as love – a space where only perfect communication, co-operation, peace and service could enter. Our destinies were joined in a common cause and it felt an honor to be a part of it.

As mentioned earlier, the question of whether or not we can predict or control the seemingly random opportunities that come our way had gradually been answered in the affirmative – that we can influence our destinies – and that this influence moves us beyond the realm of the ordinary and into the extraordinary. Success is generally measured by certain recognized criteria, such as wealth or fame. These in themselves are quite extraordinary, but when you throw in an impoverished beginning and a massively shortened time-frame, they move into the exceptional. And when you begin to recognize the connection between the metaphysical creations and their physical manifestations, a degree of trust develops.

A process of becoming

Just as we have learnt to trust in the seeming stability of the physical world, where miniscule molecules and spinning atoms behave predictability, where the tables and chairs that they form remain solidly tangible, and we don't get flung off our speedily rotating planet, so too we can learn to trust in the profound bearing of other unseen forces. As Shakespeare said, "there are more things in heaven and earth, Horatio, than are dreamt of in your philosophy".

It is only through trust that we can begin to explore beyond the borders of what we already know. Christopher Columbus would never have sailed off to the edge of the world had he not been open to question the commonly accepted view of reality and trust that he was right. (These days, sailing amongst potentially perilous coral atolls using charts from Captain Cook's time, gives me a huge sense of respect for those early pioneers.) All new discoveries have come from this willingness to step boldly forward into the unknown. When we resist moving out of our old comfort zone, nothing new can enter.

The spirit of Zen reminds us it is necessary to give up the traditional methods of reasoning, to be open to new, often seemingly paradoxical ideas, to let go and take that leap into the unknown. It is this principle of expansiveness that follows naturally upon creation. We cannot ignore our interconnectedness with all things. Through the concept of 'dependent origination', we understand that nothing exists of itself. If we try to pinpoint 'reality', the best we can say is that everything is in a process of becoming. The physical and mental self of this moment is not the same as the new-born's self that was, nor the elderly self to come. So what are we? We are certainly not the impermanent psychological processes, nor the ever-changing physical form that we so often identify ourselves with. Most of us are completely out of touch with our true nature.

The renowned Zen scholar, Alan Watts said that "True Zen is just eating when you are hungry and sleeping when you are tired." Yet how few of us do this? Our lives are much more dictated by the clock rather than natural biorhythms. When we understand Nature's laws and work with them, we are open to receive from the vast storehouse of Her abundance. The more closely we can align ourselves with our true nature, the more natural so-called miracles become and the more reliable our manifestations.

The healthy cookbook

Some of the Zen Factor strategies and techniques

take longer to do than others. It is useful to have a repertoire to choose from - in much the same way as a good cook-book offers a variety of tastes and preparation times. We might choose a fast-food 'hunger-buster' as an interim measure and then follow up with a more balanced meal later.

In the next section you will learn more strategies that can be incorporated into your own 'recipe book'. I urge you to take the time to write them out for yourself, and practice them. Without practical application they are useless. They may make interesting reading, stimulate some brief recognition and a short while later be forgotten. As you will learn, it does take some discipline and courage to proceed along this path. Fortunately these are not qualities that some have and some don't. They are available to every one of us when we choose to align ourselves with the higher energy of the all sustaining life force. You are not alone in your endeavors, unless you choose to be. Your part is to feel the fear and do it anyway. When you take the first small step you will be met and uplifted. The discipline needed to take the first step will be rewarded with an immeasurable increase in energy, so that you feel empowered to continue practicing. As mentioned earlier, when first beginning a meditation practice, it takes discipline, time and energy. But after a while, the practice itself becomes self-sustaining, and ultimately it sustains us, which is to say, it provides us with more energy than it takes.

Confidence can be developed through use. Acting *as if* we already are what we wish to be and stepping out on the skinny branches helps that confidence to grow. The things that may start out as terrifying to the novice entrepreneur such as fear of failure or the bungling of important contracts, gradually acquire less threatening dimensions. One reason for this is because over time, your worst case scenario may indeed crop up and you find that it doesn't kill you. You can survive it, take the lesson from it, and grow stronger. And as you learn that you are in fact supported by a higher intelligence, a corresponding growth in confidence follows. Then comes the humility to accept your true identity as being both a drop in the ocean as well as an energetic field that is connected to the infinite power of Creation.

SECTION III

THE WAY THINGS CAN BE

Chapter 13

The problem or the answer?

Concepts that remain just concepts, without being applied are all but useless. This book is about practical implementation rather than philosophical musing. It is easy enough to mouth abstract notions such as "don't judge", but these behaviors are so deeply ingrained as to be almost second-nature or automatic and therefore can seem very hard to alter. We are preconditioned to judge on the basis of superficial, external things, rather than to take a more compassionate stance that recognizes our unity.

An example of this was provided by a friend recently. As he was walking along a busy street, a stranger pushed him aside aggressively, using physical force and foul language to get him out of his way. The stranger did not appear to be badly dressed or under the influence of alcohol or drugs. Just an impatient man, with thoughts of himself and his mission uppermost in his mind. Many of us would have had a knee-jerk reaction to this perceived abuse, judging the man negatively and feeling ready to retaliate in the same hostile manner. Instead, my friend's inner dialogue told him he had just been accosted by a very unhappy man. His feelings were momentarily of compassion rather than retaliation, and then he dropped it and continued on his way. To hang onto something that had already disappeared and moved into the invisible world of the past, would have been to lose contact with what is in the present.

The facts of the incident had not changed – a man pushed him and swore at him. But through exercising freedom of choice on how to interpret the facts, they had lost their negative impact. By giving the experience a more compassionate interpretation, it had a completely different effect on him than had he judged harshly. To respond to the facts, with anger or even mild irritation would have been to give them power over him and in so doing, to lose his freedom and his peace.

It is only when we get to experience the direct effects of our thoughts that we begin to appreciate their full impact. We need first of all to recognize exactly what the results of our automatic behaviors are. One way or another, we can be sure that they are fear-provoking and alienating, cutting us off from everyone. It is impossible to be at peace in this situation.

So what can we do? A useful strategy is to write a memo to oneself, a symbolic reminder that we cannot judge, and place it somewhere where it is likely to be seen, such as on the fridge, the wall, the phone or on a notepad that can be carried in a pocket or bag (where we can find it). Our days can get so busy with other things that we forget what is most important. It helps to remember not only that we shouldn't judge, but that we *cannot* judge. With our limited and biased perspectives, our projected perceptions, our conditioned preconceptions and distorted paradigms, we can never know all the facts of the matter with any objectivity. But to go one step beyond this, to understand that we only hurt ourselves in the attempt to criticize or judge another, provides an even more cogent dissuasion.

It seems to be an almost unwritten law of the world that when things go wrong, someone is to blame. The hurt that we feel, quickly turns to anger. In some deeply subliminal way that we often can't even identify, we feel aggrieved, mistreated, or badly done by. This sense of injustice then demands retribution and the most immediate response is to lash out. However, the commonly selected recipient of this pent-up vengefulness is rarely the one who 'deserved' it but those closest to us; those whom we can trust to still keep on loving us no matter how much negativity we off-load on them. All too often a bad day at the office gets dumped on our loved ones at home. The ramifications of this misplaced hostility are enormous.

But if we stop and ask ourselves, who does all this furor hurt most, it will always come back to us. It is impossible to avoid. We ourselves are the victims of our own distress more than anyone else. This shows we have placed a higher value on impermanent disturbances than on our inner peace and our entire world-view represents this fearful distortion. So when molehills erupt like molten mountains, check the memo and practice equanimity. Remember, this too will pass. It is not the end of the world. There may be some important lesson to be learned from it. Or what may seem totally bad may bring some later good. You can never know. You can be sure though, that to hold onto it hurts you most of all. So take whatever lessons can be found, look for silver linings or extenuating circumstances or some other way of defusing its power over you, and then let it go. The Zen Factor tools will be of great assistance in this.

Short order strategies

Strategies are tools we use to deal with situations and we all have our favorites. It is a good idea to have at least three different strategies available and these are best prepared in advance, before the crisis hits. It is no use waiting until caught up in a situation that makes you feel like tearing your hair out – or someone else's! In the heat of the moment, stopping to count to ten, only works if it has been practiced in calmer times. So once again, practice patience, forbearance and equanimity. Practice peace-making. Practice forgiveness. These can become as much second-nature as can a quick slide into fear or anger. Which way will you go in that moment of pressure?

Another useful strategy is to ask oneself what is my desired outcome in any trying situation. What do I wish to achieve here? This needs to be a top-of the-head question and again, writing it down beforehand is useful. In times of stress we are most likely to switch to automatic pilot and react from our preconditioning. If you are the kind of person who has been well socialized, who believes in smiling nicely regardless, you will automatically dissemble rather than face an uncomfortable confrontation. The lie can be invisible to both ourselves and others, but pretence it is, and this self-deception keeps us asleep. At most it will leave a slightly bad taste, a sense of hollowness or a fleeting dejection.

It has been recognized by researchers that psychology and physiology are closely connected. The more obvious connection is from the former to the latter – when we feel dejected, we mirror that inner state in our bodies, holding ourselves in a bowed posture, wearing a frown or dull expression and generally looking miserable. The converse holds just as true: we can affect our feelings by changing our physiology. It is practically impossible to be sad whilst skipping, running, dancing or laughing out loud. Just smiling in the mirror can help lift the spirits. These are stop-gap measures to tide us over until we have the time to delve more deeply into underlying causes.

Some of the following strategies can be used in the midst of a situation involving others, some later on in the quiet of one's private sanctuary; some require longer time commitments. If it helps to group them accordingly in your personal 'recipe book of helpful strategies', do so. Here are a few of the more commonly used methods to help defuse inner turmoil:

1. Take three deep, slow breaths
2. Mentally count slowly to ten
3. Exit gracefully
4. Take a brisk walk or run
5. Put on calming or happy music
6. If you can, play music or sing
7. If you can't, learn how
8. Dance
9. Do some yoga
10. Work out at the gym

11. Play your favorite sport

12. Take a bike ride

13. Go out to a movie

14. Read a novel or an uplifting text

15. Study to learn something new

16. Go to the beach or pool

17. Visit friends – but don't talk about your problems

18. Consider other's problems and what you can do to help them

19. Write your problems down and then tear them up

20. Write down the good things in your life and stick them around the room

21. Have a shower or relaxing bath

22. Reconnect with your goals

23. And perhaps most helpful of all, sit quietly for at least ten minutes, following and counting the breath, as described in the Zen meditation. This is certain to restore inner peace in times of difficulty.

In my own experience, I found that using these strategies was a far more effective approach to dealing with problems than running around in circles making a fuss. Others respond much better to a calm appeal for help rather than panicky finger-pointing. Once a problem has arisen, the immediate need is to sort it out as quickly as possible, and this requires a team effort. A useful perspective is to see the situation as having three positions, as in the diagram below.

The problem-solving triad:

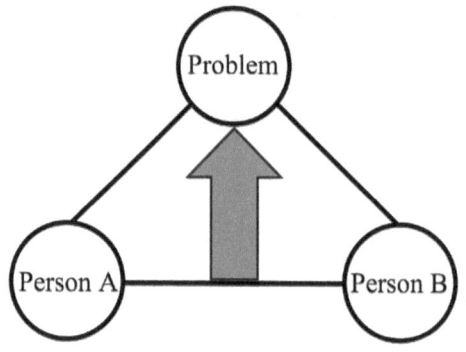

The triad represents the three elements involved: person A, person B, and the problem. But instead of having the problem placed in between the two people (or groups of people), it is removed to an external position. The three are still linked, but now in a much more conciliatory fashion, where 'You' and 'I' are united together, both facing a problem that is common to both of us. Instead of it forming a barrier between us, (as so often is the case), it has become as if a common foe. A mutually upsetting disturbance is something that we can both join forces to find solutions to. In this spirit of co-operation it is amazing how quickly satisfactory resolutions can be found. Once again, we can ask ourselves, "Do we want the problem or the answer?

Adapting

Using the Zen Factor tools for success requires great courage. It is much easier to slip back into our old ways. They are comfortable and familiar, even if perhaps a little limiting. We justify maintaining the status quo in a thousand different ways, most of all by telling ourselves it's not so bad. We have come this far without major calamity. On the surface things look all right. We allow ourselves minor transgressions of integrity such as telling little white lies or not quite telling the whole truth. We believe no-one else notices our lapses into inattention, when we have stopped listening fully. We think we can get away with small expressions of irritation or even major upheavals. We tell ourselves this is normal. This is the way everyone else is so it's OK.

But it is our ready retreat into familiar patterns and habitual behaviors that keeps us enslaved. How can we choose differently if we are unaware of the full impact of our self-deception? There are two aspects to motivation: one is movement away from something painful or undesirable; the other is movement toward something desirable. Painful experiences can thus be positive in providing us with impetus to change. We reach a point when we know this cannot continue; something has to give.

An important part of this realization is the result of having developed a more enlightened conscience. Gurdjieff refers to this sense of remorse as part of the process of "growing a conscience". This is the inner knowing that allows us to differentiate between sorrow and joy, pain and peace. When we directly feel the pain and suffering that our uncontrolled outbursts cause another, we have become more closely aligned with them. To deny this alignment is to maintain the barriers that keep us separate and therefore only capable of superficial relationships. We do this out of fear and fear is the basis of our lack of freedom.

In his book, *The Road Less Traveled*, M. Scott Peck writes of this fear of change: "When we extend ourselves, our self enters new and unfamiliar territory, so to speak. Our self becomes a new and different self. We do things we are not accustomed to do. We change. The experience of change, of unaccustomed activity, of being on unfamiliar ground, of doing things differently is frightening."

The main reason for our resistance to change is fear. Even as we begin to experience small miracles in our everyday lives, we try to dismiss them as being mere coincidence or random events that have their cause outside of us. The material world seems safe, despite its obvious threats. It is the world we have been conditioned to believe in. As we step outside of this, to a place where we are surprised by inexplicable phenomena and unlikely synchronicities, our initial reaction is to shut the door and deny their possibility. We feel on shaky ground and rush back to the old and familiar. But adaptability, or the openness and willingness to accept change, is continually being asked of us.

Are you ready to arrive?

For some people the approach of the goal can be a scary thing. A significant amount of time and energy has been invested into its realization. Heart and soul have been poured into it to such an extent that it has indeed become an extension of oneself. This is the trap to watch out for because it is very easy to become completely identified with one's own creations. Psychopathologies arise when parents fail to separate themselves from their children. The boundaries that are necessary for healthy development are never established. For the entrepreneur, the tendency is to do the same. Then it is no longer a business that I have, as much as a business that I am.

We often fall for this mistaken identification with

things we have. Our houses, cars, clothes and occupations all serve to define us and become a part of our identity. Perhaps the greatest illusion is in regard to our physical selves. I have a body, becomes I am a body. (We will look at this in more depth later). As we have seen, attachment is the root of all suffering. Somewhere around this stage I wrote in my journal entry: *"It is important to remember that the business is in my life and not vice-versa - not to get swamped by it and lost in it."* To let it go is somewhat akin to allowing one's mature offspring to venture forth alone. There is a strong temptation to cling on for longer than is in the best interests of either.

In business, arriving at the final station heralds the end - finito, game over. There is no more to be done; mission accomplished. A great sense of bathos or anticlimax can come with this. Not for everyone of course, but some will find themselves dragging their heels and resisting this fait-accomplis. They are like prisoners in an unbarred cell, fearing to step freely out. Perhaps it is time to reconnect with your original goals. Have you consciously altered them or have they slipped under cover?

Such re-evaluations of direction are very necessary. It is quite easy to forget where you were headed. On the way to buy bread you might pass the cake display and forget the bread. School children are easily distracted and have to be regularly brought back on task if they are to be taught anything. As adults we rationalize much more cleverly, having all sorts of good reasons for our new 'decisions'. Most of these justifications are simply added after the fact and are designed to cover up less noble motives, such as "I got bored with that old job/ business/ husband/ wife and find this new one much more appealing." Either way, self-deception is not only socially acceptable but actively condoned to maintain the all-important status quo.

It is fear that keeps us acting out our agreed-upon parts, long after they no longer suit us. And fear is the opposite of love, so the Zen Factor is undermined by it. The important thing is to stay true to oneself, to have the courage to admit the fear, to admit to pretence and to be 'real' instead. To be real means to own one's foibles rather than trying to conceal them. To accept whatever it is about oneself that is not so attractive or perfect. To allow oneself to simply be as one is. Even if on the outside it appears messy and not conforming to outsiders' expectations, it is important to own it and take full responsibility for it as a conscious choice we have made. Without this recognition and acceptance, we lose our authenticity, succumbing instead to a more passive, victim mode of thinking.

Never underestimate the power of the ego to

resist change and to keep you bound by its rules. It has an endless repertoire of sticky little ways of keeping us small and asleep. An enormous degree of vigilance is required to spot its control over every little thing. This means developing a mindset of curiosity, being interested, paying attention and refusing to be soft on yourself. When our primary intent is personal development, mastery of self and freedom, we need all the help we can get to rise above our fears. To quote M. Scott Peck again: "Courage is not the absence of fear; it is the making of action in spite of fear, the moving out against the resistance engendered by fear into the unknown and into the future."

Chapter 14

The trail to now

It is fair to say that we are essentially self-serving creatures and will generally operate in what seems to be our own best interest. Any endeavor we might undertake must satisfy that need. On the surface, it can appear that many of our actions are quite the opposite, often bordering on sabotage or self-destruction. Invariably however, we will find some deeply buried motivation behind these counter-productive behaviors that is in fact self-serving. We will always move toward pleasure and away from pain, taking the path of least resistance, i.e. the most well-worn, best known path. While the resultant behavior may not be the most rational, on some level it has been chosen as the best available to satisfy the deeper need. We need to recognize that whatever we do, we ourselves choose to do it and that we make that choice because it is the one that satisfies us most. There are many levels to this choosing.

If we keep asking ourselves the question, "and what does that give me?" we will eventually get down to a core need, such as peace or happiness. To satisfy that objective we instinctively direct our lives in ways that we believe are away from pain and toward pleasure. If pressures at work are building up, an illness or car accident can provide some respite. Whilst it is still painful, it is considered by the subconscious to be a lesser evil and doesn't involve the same stresses. It should be becoming clear that this modus operandi needs closer examination as it can lead us down some dark holes.

No change can be made in the present if its cause is in the past and if this is left unquestioned. To give an example, a woman I know had been suffering from agoraphobia, the inability to be alone outdoors, for over three and a half years. At first sight this condition appears to be utterly debilitating and in no way self-serving. However, with further delving, an earlier experience emerged that provided sound reasons for her present behavior. The belief she had formed from this was that going outside was potentially life-threatening and she was much safer to avoid it. Becoming aware of this connection can sometimes be sufficient to understand the cause of the present problem and see it for its irrationality.

"A Course In Miracles" tells us that memory is equally as selective as perception, being its past tense. This thin slice of a 'reality' that has been formed by a selectively remembered past is often used in a way that holds the present to ransom. But there are any number of different perspectives and different conclusions that can

be drawn from any recollection. Once we shed light on these distorted views they become much more available for us to re-consider and question their validity. If our ultimate aim is to have peace of mind then it is important to be vigilant against errors of perception.

A Unified Self

In recent times, a lot has been written about the power of affirmations, where all a person needs to do to attain the fulfillment of their heart's desires is to write down what it is they want. To a certain extent this is true, however there is rather more to it, as we have already seen. Each of the elements of the Zen Factor contributes to the holistic fullness of tapping into such creative powers. Perhaps the most basic precursor of these is the starting point of what I call a 'Unified Self'.

Let me give an example: John Smith has been a heavy smoker for the past twelve years. He suffers the usual corollaries of this; the sore throats, hacking cough, breathlessness, not to mention the ever-more-heavily-advertised health risks of diabetes, emphysema, cancer, heart attack or other cardiovascular diseases. He knows what is at stake. His family and friends have been on at him for years about it, so finally he decides to quit.

It has taken a lot to come to this point but at

last he feels he is ready to tackle it. He is psyched up, pumped and ready for battle. Just before going to bed on Monday night he throws out his cigarettes, lighters, ash-trays and takes a long shower. He is brimming with all the self-confidence of an evangelist and feels full of virtuous strength.

But come Tuesday morning a different John Smith wakes up. All that heady confidence and strong resolve has vanished. In fact, it feels to John as if someone else made that decision, not him. A mass rebellion is going on inside of him. His whole body is craving a smoke. Sure, he knew it would be hard; he knew to expect some cravings and that he would have to grin and bear it until it passed. But the big difference on Tuesday morning is that he doesn't really want to quit anymore. It is as if there are several different selves in there, with different agendas and different desires. And more often than not, they are not in communication with each other at all. The self that made the decision to quit on Monday night is in no way related to the self that woke up on Tuesday morning. They might just as well be living in foreign countries on opposite sides of the world, speaking completely different languages.

We have all had this experience in some way or another and usually place the blame for our failures on something like 'lack of will-power'. But a general axiom is that 'where there is need for will, there is lack of skill.' If we try and force ourselves into a different shape through the sheer force of our will, an enormous amount of energy is required to overcome the inevitable resistance that arises to counter this. It truly is as if a battle is going on inside us. The self that is dominant will be the one that quashes the others. But to quell any part of ourselves is to cause tension and takes energy to sustain. A far better approach is through the ease of a unified self.

Our Higher Self

When we get in touch with who it is that we really are, we see there is in fact only one self, call it if you wish our higher Self. This is the self that is connected to the universal intelligence that can never be separated from the whole, nor split into different aspects of itself. There can never be a struggle to unify the seemingly discrete parts once there is recognition of their cohesiveness - any more than the drop of water could struggle to become the ocean or any of our billions of cells could exist apart from the whole. When we are not in touch with this reality, we can only see ourselves as separate individuals, each one separate from the other, split from our source and divided within ourselves.

We often hear people say things like, "a part of

me wants this, but another part of me wants that." This is a sign of imbalance and confusion, which taken to extreme is diagnosed as the condition of schizophrenia or split personality. "I want to eat healthily but I also love junk food" is a more commonly heard dichotomy, which is considered quite normal. In this more normal scenario, an apparent 'truce' is achieved, according to whichever 'I' is getting its way at the moment, that is to say, while the other 'I' is being silenced, ignored or subjugated.

A far more potent reconciliation is possible, where both parts are brought together, respectfully acknowledging their contribution to the deeper, self-serving aim. As mentioned above, this will generally be a core need, such as peace, happiness or love. We all have a core need to feel connected. At this level there is seldom any conflict to be found. As always, it is self-awareness that is the key. In times of stress, our underlying motives can be very deeply buried. It can take a major upheaval to make us sit up and take notice and sometimes we unwittingly orchestrate those ourselves. Life has its twists and turns, its shifts in and out of reason and reasonableness. As we have seen, sometimes seemingly unreasonable actions can be to gain something that we believe will bring us happiness, or at least to avoid something we believe is worse.

Choose again

Do we choose the seemingly random events that occur in our lives? To explain this we generally look for some rationale based on personal gain. It seems illogical to actively choose something harmful. Yet we have seen that quite often people's behaviors can be distorted beyond anything that might be deemed positive, while still being self-serving. One thing is for certain, we can choose how we respond to life's challenges and it is this that provides us with either peace or suffering. It is when we rail against the hand we believe we have been dealt, refusing to accept any responsibility for it, that we become the victim and suffer accordingly.

We don't actually need to ascribe any particular reason at all to our choosing; it is enough to simply recognize that 'this is what I chose'. No matter what it is, no matter how bizarre or seemingly incongruous, taking responsibility for it is a way of reclaiming our power as causative agents in our own lives. This is a first step toward freedom. Even apparent catastrophes can contain valuable lessons and looking at them in this light alters the way in which we see ourselves. We begin to move away from the belief that 'bad stuff just happens to me for no apparent reason'.

It has been said that there is no such thing as an

accident, though when one happens, it can be hard to see how that could be so. But if we consider the possibility of a self-serving motivation, we can see that even things that seem to be the last thing we would want to happen may in fact be chosen. In the words of *"A Course in Miracles"*, "Everything that seems to happen to me I ask for and receive as I have asked." This is a tough idea to accept and requires paying much closer attention to the well-concealed evidence.

Things appear to change suddenly, because that is the essence of change; it happens in the present moment. There may have been many years of groundwork being laid beforehand, with each of the steps having been taken in the then present time. Often a path of our choosing can be so far removed from the initial steps as to be unrecognizable. Take, for example, the likelihood of a major illness suddenly cropping up out of nowhere. How likely does this seem? One day we are perfectly healthy, with nothing simmering away beneath the surface, and then, bang, diabetes. No pre-existing conditions, no predisposition, no pre-determinants – and of course it has nothing at all to do with diet or lifestyle. No responsibility. Or consider a marriage breakdown – one day everything going along just fine and then, crash, divorce. Or a career failure, or alienated children or a lonely old-age. The list could go on. Have they simply happened, for no apparent reason? Most of these events are results that have been a long time in the making. Consider each of these as a result of a myriad of causes - physical, emotional, psychoneuroimmunological - and we begin to see the trail to now.

It is not always possible to know all the facts of the matter, or which branch of which cross-road will lead to where we are meant to be. Sometimes the most unlikely path can bring us to a place that is exactly right for us. Then there is an alignment of forces that creates ease and harmony. The evidence for this is in our sense of peace and an inner knowing that this is 'right'. We can always tell when we are off-track, when things stick, grate, or don't flow smoothly. Then it is likely that we are putting up a fight, trying to block the river or make it flow upstream. If we cling to the past and resist change, we cause ourselves undue suffering. Letting go and letting be is the gentler course.

Good luck or bad?

The 'butterfly effect' is a term used to describe the unknowable influence that small things can have on larger outcomes. It presumes we can never know in advance which way things might turn out, or for whom any one particular set of circumstances is 'good luck' or 'bad luck'. There are many stories of this in Zen literature, the moral of all of them being the same: that what might appear to be 'bad' can turn out to be 'good' and vice-versa. So it is best to remain unaffected by whatever happens, or at least to let go and regain one's equilibrium as quickly as possible.

You may have read this tale before: In a small village, the venerated Zen master Hakuin was accused of being the father of a young woman's illegitimate child. "If you say so," he answered. All of his followers reviled him for this moral transgression, and chose to abandon him. He was given the child to raise alone, which he did with as much love and care as any natural father might give. A year later, the child's mother confessed that it was not Hakuin, but some other man who was in fact the father. Her parents came and took the child back from the monk, who as before, only replied to their claims, "if you say so." How many of us could show the same calm acceptance in such circumstances? Most of us would add all kinds of interpretations to the fact, causing ourselves extra suffering. To be able to accept what is, in the present moment, without attachment or judgment, only comes from a position of freedom.

In operating your own business you will find many opportunities to practice non-attachment to external circumstances. Every day small problems may arise that seem to have been deliberately planted just to annoy you. Your tolerance may be down through tiredness or hunger, or troubles at home. We all have our 'off' days when we are more likely to take the bait and become overly reactive. At such times we can slip into a downward spiral, perceiving insult heaped upon injury, so that at the end of the day we are questioning why we are here; why do we have to put up with all this stress?

When minor irritations mount up, one upon the other, each assumes a greater importance than they have alone. The inefficiency of colleagues becomes annoying. They are not listening. They are not being the way we want them to be. Procedures that have been well-defined are suddenly forgotten. Expectations need to be lowered, but we are not feeling flexible right now. We look around for causes of our distress outside of ourselves. Those who cause us continuing grief we label and store.

A grievance is an idea of a wrong-doing that is held onto as a reminder of some injustice done to us in the past. We believe it deserves space in our memory banks, 'lest we forget'. This keeps us on our guard, moving with caution and reserve. We can never be completely at ease.

The generally held belief is that 'time will heal'; but this is not accurate. For some people, time never heals; they hold onto grievances forever. Others get over things more quickly. In reality, it takes no time to let go of a grievance. How? Through forgiveness. Through understanding that we are not an impermanent body, or a thought, or anything that can be hurt. Through staying in the present moment. It takes the recognition that to hold onto a grievance hurts us more than it hurts anyone else. It takes a bigger self, capable of overlooking mistakes, capable of seeing that we are not separate, warring aspects, but all part of the one whole. There are times when this seems almost impossible; but if we make even the smallest effort in that direction, the universe will bend to meet us, gather us up and offer all the help we need to be at peace again.

The small quiet voice

To love our life is to be happy with it, in all respects. There is no room for fear, grievances or anger. These things destroy love. Even the tiniest, scarcely recognized irritation, a slight raising of the eyebrows or rolling of the eyes, provide the hint that illusions are knocking at the door. The precursors of anger seem tame enough in these mild disguises, yet they quickly grow to choke the Garden of Eden. If we would know a complete and all-inclusive inner peace we must beware of the tone of lament. How often, even in casual exchanges, do we allow ourselves some slight complaint over something seemingly inconsequential, like the weather, our aches and pains, our partners, our children, our working environment, colleagues or bosses? It all seems harmless enough, yet were we to see the impact even such trivial thoughts or comments were having on us and on our world, we might re-think it and choose again. Shakespeare's quote: "sufficient unto the day is the evil thereof" comes to mind, and although I don't like his use of the word 'evil', I understand that there is enough going on in the present, not to be worrying about what 'evil' there might be lurking in the future.

The small, quiet voice is something rarely heard in our noisy minds. It is completely different from the haphazard thoughts that arise in our normal inner voice, having a more directive quality and certainty about it. There may be a dialogue which is suggesting alternative ways of approaching things. If the suggested path is followed, it leads to peace. M. Scott Peck describes such guidance that came to him when at his lowest ebb: "At the moment of my greatest despair, from my unconscious came a sequence of words, like a strange disembodied oracle from a voice that was not mine: *"The only real security in life lies in relishing life's insecurity."*" Wise words indeed.

Sadly, our habit is to ignore this guidance in preference for the autocratic voice of the ego; one we guard as if something precious. This is the voice we are most familiar with and our ears are attuned to. Its ramblings are rarely cohesive yet we have placed our trust in it completely. Following this rambunctious ruler, we can easily be led astray. In order to become a more conscious being, we must be vigilant, paying attention to which inner voice we are heeding.

7 steps for reclaiming peace

Each step we take, each moment we take it, moves us toward or away from something and reflects the choices we are making in each of those moments. To reverse the direction, to choose again, we need to realize that what is, is part of a process of becoming. Even so, it is possible to choose again in the present moment, and quite often this is enough to undo the chains and start afresh. A useful tool for this reclamation is via the following seven step process:

1. Relax, clear the mind and enter the place of stillness

2. Contemplate the present state of disturbance

3. Consider the process that formed the chain of events

4. Find the very first step that began the process

5. Do not judge; see that 'it is what it is'

6. Acknowledge: "I have chosen wrongly and choose again"

7. Visualize the alternative path that might now ensue.

As always, all the senses need to be brought to bear in the visualization. In this way we can correct our errors of perception, choose to have the answer rather than the problem, let go and move on.

"A Course in Miracles" reminds us: "There is a way of finding certainty right here and now. Refuse to be a part of fearful dreams, whatever form they take, for you will lose your identity in them. You find yourself by not accepting them as causing you and giving you effects."

Again, it is necessary to be vigilant, so we can notice when these 'fearful dreams' begin. We can nip them in the bud before they take hold, grow bigger and develop into monsters. When we control our minds, we control our world. Or the same idea can be rephrased: when we are free of our limiting beliefs, we can create a life we love. It is always possible to choose again.

Chapter 15

Redefining success

Many people believe that money will buy them happiness, but money for its own sake can be fraught with the 'evil' that is sometimes associated with it. There are innumerable examples to be found where abundant wealth has not brought contentment. More often it has generated misery through the constant pressure to keep hold of it or to see it multiply. A multi-billionaire couple I know live in the most degrading state of hostility, each making the other's life hell on account of the wealth that comes between them. Despite having infinitely more income and stockpiles than either could ever use, they protect their individual fortunes with their very lives.

It seems that once a high level of opulence has been reached, the thought of losing it can become unbearable. The safeguard against loss is to have more; and more again. The taint of money is in this fear and grasping. No matter how much there is it is as if there is never enough. This is the way of the small-hearted, small-minded, miserly person who is totally enslaved by their fears.

Return again to the pie graph at the beginning of

this book, which asked you to contemplate the different sectors in your life and consider the varying measures of success. The new business paradigm is moving away from financial wealth as the primary arbiter of having made it in society. Success is personal and dynamic, shifting with the different stages of our lives. Added to the list of criteria are now things like personal growth, contribution, inner freedom, peace and happiness. A deeper connection with others, with self and with everything that exists both independently and dependently is present. There is creativity, expansion and largesse. A sense of gratitude to the higher power that guides us gently toward our greatest good is present. Attachment to worldly possessions falls away.

The spectrum of possibilities

Greed may be defined as coveting, grasping, or clinging to what we have and wanting more than what is sufficient. Of course everyone will have a different idea of what is sufficient. For some, a roof over the head and food on the table is enough. Many of the so-called primitive peoples on earth have only this and yet are the happiest. They have a high regard for family and community that gives them a sense of belonging. Oral histories link them to their ancestors and heritage. They live in communally-built houses, work in family gardens and cook together over fires in shared 'kitchens'. If a cyclone destroys the village, they all pitch in to rebuild it. If a child's mother dies, another mother, perhaps related, will take it in, suckle it and raise it amongst her own. The children's laughter can be heard throughout the villages and it is rare to find a sultry or malcontent adolescent. Without outside influence, they live happily in the present, not rebelling against authority or wanting for more than they have.

To an extent then, happiness is culturally bound and will be influenced by the living standards of those around us. If everyone has the same and there is no obvious disparity between rich and poor, there is little discontent, aside from the normal tribulations of daily life. These challenges are dealt with as they arise and don't leave lingering residues, as is the case in our culture. But while we may miss out on these utopian lifestyles, we have gained the opportunity to exercise more control over our own destinies. It is possible for us to have the best of both worlds.

For those of us born into Western civilization in so-called 'first world' countries, there is a vast range of possibilities open to us, from poverty to enormous wealth. We can choose where we fit in the spectrum. This is a liberty of our time and place and one that is quite unique in our history. Never before has the slide been so slippery, the possibilities so open. This flexibility of our era is another fortune of happenstance, and one which we can use to our benefit. We are not culturally bound by our beginnings anymore; we can set our sights high, aim for the stars and leave our past behind. As I have heard said, "money can't buy you happiness; but it can buy you a big enough boat to sail right up to it!"

Of course, like every double-ended stick, this freedom brings its own challenges. Never before have we had so many choices available to us. Never before have we been asked to take so much responsibility. The peasant's life is clearly defined, from birth to death. His or her place in society is set and not open to question. There is a certain comfort and security comes with this pre-established order. There is no crescendo or hiatus, no depression that follows on absence of direction or cause. So we are at once blessed and damned by our civilization, free to reap its benefits and free to suffer its black holes, according to our own choices.

Context

It helps to remember that we ourselves provide the meaning in our lives. We can choose how we interpret events. Consider for example, the completely different responses we might have to the same situation: we wake up alone. This could be because our partner has gone to work early, or has taken a short business trip, or has left us. Each scenario displays the same manifestation (present); yet each would be experienced differently according to the background causes (past) and anticipated ramifications to come (future). If these are ignored, we are left with only the present moment to deal with. But we cannot easily ignore the context that surrounds isolated facts. We might even question if there is any such thing as an isolated fact.

Meaning is both contextual and consensual. Things don't happen in a vacuum. They occur within a context, having a particular set of circumstances surrounding them from which we draw inferences. These help us to know how to respond to any given situation. I have memories of difficult periods in my life, when I have had no idea of how I was meant to be in response to the situation.

Similarly, the consensus of others' opinions has a bearing on our interpretations of events. For example, the fact that it is raining today might be considered annoying because an outdoor concert has been planned. The same rainy day might be welcomed enthusiastically following a long period of drought. Most of our assessments will divide things into 'good' or 'bad'. Those things that warm us, feed us, protect us are considered good; those that hurt, sting or bite us are bad. It is in our nature to ascribe meaning. We might be described as 'meaning-making machines'. But it is important to remember that the tags we use to make sense of our world are rather arbitrary devices. They serve a purpose in uniting us in a rationalized manner based on the conventions we have agreed upon. In themselves, they are nothing. The events they describe are quite neutral and have no independent meaning in isolation.

The test for peace

When something happens, the natural response is to question: "what does it mean?" It is very difficult for us to simply accept that something happened, and leave it at that. We need to be able to pin one of our labels on it, which will tell us if it is good or bad, safe or threatening. This will tell us how we should react to it. Should we laugh or cry? Should we stay or run? Meanings are definitely useful for our survival, but we should be aware of when we are being enslaved by them, when they are not helpful.

The test for this is always the same: where is our inner peace? Are we anxious or calm? When we are agitated or distressed, or caught up in any other more subtle disturbance, we can be sure that we have become lost in an unhelpful mindset. Any form of identification with anything is bound to unsettle us. Identification occurs when we have lost ourselves in something to such an extent that it has become as if a part of us. If it is taken away from us we are certain that we will suffer loss. 'It' can be a thing, a person, an idea, or a particular meaning we have attributed to any of these.

Usually it is not the thing, person, or idea that causes us trouble, but the meaning we have added. For example, some might think, 'if my lover doesn't return a call, it means s/he doesn't love me anymore'; 'if my boss criticizes my work, it means s/he doesn't like me personally', and so on. The important thing to remember in all this is that the world we see does nothing in itself. It simply represents our thoughts. We have looked inwardly first, before assessing what is going on outwardly. We have measured whatever it is we encounter in the world against the preconceived notions we hold onto about it. This makes it impossible to experience what is, as it truly is, right now.

A thought about some imminent meeting with a difficult person can upset our equilibrium now, yet that thought is nothing in itself. Of itself it cannot harm us, unless we let it. By inviting it into our minds and allowing it full play, we create mischief for ourselves. It certainly appears to be real and reasonable to react to it as if it were. We feel quite justified in giving rein to these worries. To us they seem to be inextricably connected to the reality of their external causes. But are they really? Or are we spinning stories and looking for meaning, where none exists in the natural *isness* of things. Even more insidious is the belief that we are our thoughts and have no control over them.

The thinking process

Thoughts certainly do seem to be a part of ourselves to such an extent that we often mistakenly identify ourselves with them. It is hard for us to realize that we are separate from our thoughts and that they are separate from us and can even come from outside of us. Let us consider for a moment the machinations of our inner world. What is the process? What is going on in there? At times we might struggle to recall something, an event, a place or name. Is 'struggle' the right word? What does that imply – that our brain cells are whirring about inside our heads, busily searching through billions of connections that certain synapses have laid down in the past, the neuronal pathways to which have long been lost?

This might conjure up an image of infinite rows of dusty old filing cabinets packed full of useless snippets of information - filed away for future reference; stored away in the deep dark recesses of the mind; gone but not entirely forgotten. And then the day comes when some particular bit is wanted. Something else nudges up close to it, causing a faint recollection, but not quite the whole story. Just an echo that reminds you of.... but no, you can't quite grasp it. You know it's there. How do you know? You haven't seen it in ages, but you know that you know. It's clear that there is a mechanism for knowing whether you know or don't know something and whether there is any point in looking for it or not. So you begin searching through the archives, the dusty and then the even dustier ones. In some way, it does feel like a strain, not quite like using a muscle, but still a strain. Hence the concept of struggling to remember. Your mind jags off in pursuit of logical connections, but usually that is a blind alley. It is more likely that the required information will somehow simply come to you.

Take for example an occasion when I was trying to recollect the name of a well-known comedian. Something prompted the search; one of his lines cropped up in conversation. But what was his name? This was not going to be top-of-the-head information, because I had only ever seen a couple of his performances and that was several years ago. And even then, I didn't take all that much notice of his name. It wasn't that important. Yes, another factor in the shelving process is importance, or ongoing relevance. If it's important, like for instance, one's own phone number, then it's more likely to be filed very close by. But what does that mean? Close by to what? In a computer's CPU (or Central Processing Unit) are there things stored closer to the centre or more to the periphery - and which is the quicker access point? And is the brain like a CPU? That would be rather a mechanistic view, difficult to reconcile here. Remember Candace Pert's conclusion that thoughts do not even arise in the brain, which is just the hardware for electrical impulses.

So I set about searching, though I have no idea how. How does one search one's mind for information? What is the process? And even more interesting is the fact that I can watch myself search my mind. How can I *be* my mind or my thoughts if I can watch this activity? I can certainly feel the effort. At times it almost hurts! It is not something one can sustain for very long. Nor should one. In most cases it's not that important. And quite apart from that, there is a better way. The better way is to leave it alone. Set the wheels in motion then sit back and wait. Now this is a very curious phenomenon. The mind will continue the search alone. There is an intelligence within that is able to direct it autonomously, a kind of seek and find function that persists unaided. It is seen in Archimedes' famous exclamation of "Eureka" at the sudden, unexpected solution to a problem.

In this instance however, I was sitting in quiet meditation with no light-bulbs flashing above my head. I had been practicing "ask and ye shall receive" meditation, asking to be raised to a higher level of consciousness. I have found this to be a very worthwhile practice and each time I asked, I instantly felt myself raised up. While at that higher level, I thought, just for fun, why not ask what that elusive name was? I asked, and immediately, a voice in my head supplied the required information. Instant recognition! Where did that come from? Certainly not through the usual channels. Rather, as in so many other instances of asking, obscure information becomes available in quietude. How does that happen? It seems we can't pull ourselves up by our own bootlaces. But we can ask for help from the miracle of our connected minds. This is one of the most useful tools available to us when the confusion of multiple possibilities overwhelms us in our business decision-making process.

Chapter 16

Acts of creation

As discussed earlier, an entrepreneur is someone involved in creation who is operating out of service and love. It stands to reason that no-one would want to create something that wasn't as beautiful, functional and perfect as it could possibly be. Creation is an act of expansion and extension. Through the expansiveness of creation, we extend ourselves into the world in much the same way as when we reproduce ourselves through our offspring. We naturally love our creations and strive to do all we can for them. The idea of service carries no sense of effort or hardship because it is a reciprocal feeding, each of the other. There are many more ways of 'feeding' than simply eating food. Higher energies feed us and as they do, they themselves are increased. Contained within every act of service is an instantaneous reciprocation; giving automatically includes receiving.

Recently I asked a friend of mine which part of his job he enjoyed most. Without hesitation he said it was the pleasure of giving the best possible service to customers. He enjoyed the friendly chats, the good humor and laughter that he was able to elicit from practically everyone he dealt with and the knowledge that he had contributed in some small way to lightening up their day. He loved the interactions of enquiry into their needs and the satisfaction of supplying what they were looking for. Most of all he felt good when they felt good. Making the sale was secondary to the process of giving excellent service. He described it as a win-win-win-win-win situation, where he, the customer, the boss, the store and the company all win.

In order to deliver this kind of service, your own energy levels need to be high. When you have taken the time to practice the Zen Factor techniques you will find yourself becoming naturally high. As we have already seen, it takes a lot of energy to suppress things deeply within ourselves and to construct a false identity. It is a constant effort to deny our true selves, to hide, shield and put up barriers between ourselves and others. As we practice removing the blocks to the awareness of our true selves we lighten up, become more energized, and able to raise the vibrations of others. We become more attractive, like a magnetic force.

Like attracts like

As a business grows it brings the opportunity to hire like-minded people who hold similar values and who will be fun to work with. Such people bring vitality, enthusiasm and the higher energy of those who are connected to reality. They live more fully in the present moment and are free to respond to its needs in precisely appropriate ways. Joline Godfey has written extensively on this in her book *"Our Wildest Dreams"*:

"Fun companies are full of alive, vital people. They have a gleam in their eyes – a sense of mischievous daring about them. The air around them is often electric. Tasks are accomplished, and products, both tangible and intangible, are shipped out the door. Industry is palpable. Just under the surface is the life force that keeps it happening. Inherent in that life force is a large element of playfulness and adventure."

For the entrepreneur, the success of your enterprise will be closely connected to the kind of workplace environment you create. People are involved, and people are complex beings. If whole people are to be welcome in your business, then it needs to be recognized that they come with many facets, bringing laughter and sadness, creativity and moodiness, imagination and dreaming. When you pick up a stick, you pick up both ends, not just the good end or the useful part. When whole people are encouraged, you get to know both sides of the coin and you need to be comfortable with this. Occasionally you may need to lend a sympathetic ear, or allow time off for some crisis or personal need. The trade-off is that all kinds of diverse talents and skills become available.

Everyone can contribute something to the success of the whole and this something may be a hitherto unrecognized talent or perspective. The more different perspectives available the better. Then the business grows like an organic entity in its own right, feeding off the unique input that each part contributes to its growth. It begins to take on a life of its own that you know can exist apart from you and from others who have fed it along the way. It becomes a self-sustaining force, developing the strength to rise above all obstacles.

Difficulties are a load that can be lightened by a unified approach, as seen in the triad example given earlier. When the problem is placed externally to the observers they can then work together to understand what is needed to solve it. No-one owns the problem or identifies with it or allows it to stand between them and others. If problems are faced together rather than in opposition solutions are more easily found. Within this conciliatory and collaborative model obstacles become challenges which are opportunities for growth. We can introduce more inspired ways of looking at things. We can question our habitual behaviors and preconditioned assumptions. Work ethics in particular are deeply ingrained in our culture, reinforcing the notion of work *then* play, rather than work and play.

We have already observed that the more traditional business models are likely to be triangular in shape, with the controllers at the apex ruling the worker-drones at the base. There is no collaboration between the various levels in the hierarchy. All decision making is autocratic, based on the assumption that those at the top know best and that leaders direct followers. There is no appreciation for the potential contribution of the underlings, who are regarded purely and simply as having been employed to fulfill a set task. They are not expected to provide any feedback or input. There is no upward communication other than complaint, and this is more often than not disregarded.

Work and play

While it is true that there needs to be strong leadership, this needn't preclude contribution from others. Quite often, various members of staff will have profound observations to make on the state of affairs at the ground level and these should be encouraged. In the circular business model, people pull together as part of a team. Their opinions are respected and valued. An employee assessment form might include things like productivity, meeting set targets, contribution to decision-making, team-building, taking responsibility, overcoming difficulties, relationships with co-workers, attitude to work, and capacity for fun. Fun can be seen as either disruptive and threatening or as adaptive and expansive. People need to feel safe enough to play a little within the structures of stability. When my children were young, a lot of our play was held within the bounds of what I called 'organized chaos'. This is a useful way of maintaining the necessary balance between safety and alertness, work and play. Obviously different types of establishments will have varying capacities for allowing zaniness.

One highly successful company operating out of South Africa has questions around the idea of fun on its employee assessment form. How much fun are you having at work? Do others find you fun to be around? Do you contribute to a positive atmosphere? Are you aware of what you are doing? Do you enjoy what you are doing? Such questions let everyone know that this company cares about other things than simply the numeric bottom line, although that too will be blossoming.

When the workplace is a fun place to be and people enjoy being there, they are more likely to be aligned with the higher values and overall vision of the enterprise. They can feel free to express themselves honestly without fear of ridicule. This is the case when laughter is always *with*, never *at*. A healthy work environment hears the kind of spontaneous laughter that treasures diversity and is not based on put-downs or having fun at another's expense. It is vital to encourage an ethos of mutual respect between all team members at every level. Everyone can be respected for what they bring, no matter how quirky or different. Daring to be different is the fuel of great discoveries.

Creating a healthy workplace

The sky is the limit when it comes to imagining the kind of environment that you and others would enjoy working in. What would such a place look like, sound like, or feel like? Would there be people actively engaged in conversation, sharing ideas, being engrossed in set tasks, taking regular breaks to stretch a little, perhaps occasionally sitting in deep contemplation? Or would they be glued to their work-station, watching the clock, counting the minutes until knock off? Would personality clashes flare up from time to time? Would the general energy level be of torpor, sluggish and weak?

To imagine something better begins with redefining the word 'work' which carries so many connotations of boredom, dreariness, or the pain of suffering through the daily grind. It is not easy for us to change this image for one of light-heartedness, fun, laughter, or any of the things we normally associate with the word 'play'. Centuries of collective agreement have formed our view. If we are shown a picture of a person staring absently into space and asked the question, are they working? most would say no. There are no outwardly visible displays of activity. Yet that supposed daydreamer may be inventing something of massive importance. If we frown upon down-time, contemplation or lateral thinking we will be left with obliging serfs who do only what is required of them - and that to the minimum. To change this mindset requires active use of the Zen Factor tools that have been described throughout this book. Remember, the one thing you can change is your mind. It is possible to create anew.

Seven more tools

To reiterate a model of a successful business, it looks something like this: there is the creation of innovative ideas, services or high quality products which provide benefit to others. Amongst the staff, there is a sense of purpose, integrity and contribution through relationships which are mutually supportive. There is an ethos of exceptional service, above and beyond expectations. An atmosphere of consideration, trust and co-operation exists, with provision for life's demands as well as for fun. There is open communication with the utmost respect always being shown. There is no dichotomy of work versus life; money versus time, self versus other, or work before play. Laughter abounds. Business and pleasure can be mixed.

Here are seven ways to assist in imagining/creating a healthy workplace:

1. Appreciation. We all like to feel appreciated and this can be fostered through acknowledgement of achievements. All of the items mentioned above in the staff assessment criteria can be used to offer awards, such as formal presentation of certificates of appreciation, or rewards such as bonuses, movie or theatre tickets, weekend retreats at health resorts or exclusive hotels, or a fine dining experience. Milestones such as anniversaries of key events in the business can be celebrated. In fact, as we have already noted, it is vitally important to do so, providing opportunities to stop and give thanks for the progress made and gifts received. Opportunities to show heartfelt appreciation and gratitude are everywhere.

2. Be a consistent role-model. No trust can be developed if you are inconsistent in your expectations and in your own behavior. If you wish to encourage fun but frown upon outbursts of frivolity you will create confusion and reticence. Set the example in the same way as a parent sets to children, by being the change you wish to see. If you demonstrate anger, frustration or impatience that is what you will receive. Using the tools of the Zen Factor, model patience, understanding and equanimity. Discuss these ideals as well as the short and long-term goals and allow others to add tips from their own experience. Encourage participation in goal-setting exercises and self-awareness tools.

3. Environment. Brainstorm various ways in which to create an environment that's conducive to engendering positive energy, unification of effort and innovative spirit. Use walls and desks for displaying inspirational calendars, posters, signs, place-mats, drawings or cartoons. Include vibrant colors in the decor, let in fresh air and natural light and grow living plants. If possible, provide a quiet space for short intervals of respite, contemplation or meditation. These breaks can be highly energizing ways of recharging batteries, seeking inspiration or finding exactly what the next step is. Often it pays to walk away from something for a while to allow new perspectives or inspiration to enter. A quiet room can use dimmed lighting, beautiful artworks, floral displays and soothing music to create an uplifting space.

4. Play-school policies. In schools, children are given regular breaks during classroom activities to revive their attention-span, keep them awake, focused and enjoying their learning. Children naturally enjoy learning new things and teachers are trained to make this as enjoyable as possible for them within the structure of an organized curriculum. Teaching aids are often like toys that facilitate learning through play. It is well recognized that a head, hands and heart approach achieves best results. The transition from school to work leaves all this behind, which is a great shame. At very least, encourage regular breaks, changes in activity and some kind of physical exercise. Stretching is a great reviver.

5. Movement matters. Heed the examples of others (from whatever field) who are successfully doing what you wish to do. Workers in China are taken outside at the start of their working day to do physical exercises, which increases productivity. Yoga postures are good for improving focus, calmness and inner fortitude. An almost instant reviver is the practice of alternate nostril breathing, which helps connect right and left brain function. This is done by placing the index and middle fingers slightly above the bridge of the nose, closing off the right nostril with the thumb while inhaling through the left nostril, then releasing that, closing the left nostril with the ring finger and exhaling through the right nostril. Inhale through that nostril and continue alternating for a few cycles. Check what people are comfortable with before offering specific things. Encourage written input of suggestions via a feedback box or on a large whiteboard that is not used for business schedules or timelines.

6. Give back. Several businesses show that they value

their people by providing subsidized or free meals, having a masseur visit, offering gym membership and personal fitness programs, giving a day off for birthdays, organizing group outings or taking an annual retreat to somewhere beautiful. Demonstrating value needn't be extravagant or hugely expensive; it can be something as simple as inviting a storyteller or artist or some other entertainer, perhaps from your own network. It is enough to convey the message that you value the contribution of each and every one and wish to reciprocate in some way beyond the usual.

7. Commit to fun. Most of all, hold in high regard a dedicated commitment to fun and look for ways to share it. Regularly ask the question, what fun things can we do today? Having staff is like having playmates on hand every day. Enjoy their company, joke together and encourage moments of play in passing. Things won't collapse into a heap in even the most serious of businesses for the odd witty comment. If humorous ad-libbing isn't your forte, look for funny stories to relate or have a stash of joke books on hand.

There are innumerable ways of committing to fun. If you pay attention, you will find many opportunities to bring forth warmth and happiness, and in so doing, be a part of raising the vibrational energy of our planet and all of its occupants. Notice how smiles linger long after their cause. Hearts are warmed and that warmth spreads. We need more of it.

If only for a few minutes each day, look for ways of lifting energy and spreading joy. Perhaps throw out a few brain teasers or lateral thinking puzzles. You could turn evening brainstorming sessions into fun by serving great meals from international cuisines. Or announce time-out to go down to the local pool for a swim beforehand. The unexpected always lifts our spirits. Each day introduce different possibilities for lightening the atmosphere. Maybe hold a favorite recipe bake-off, a limerick writing competition or a movie theme dress-up. How about borrowing some children's games to play whilst taking a picnic rug outside for lunch? Be daring. Laugh easily and freely. Risk the embarrassment of looking silly. It may take time to develop the trust but soon the inner child will feel comfortable enough to come out to play. Nurture this precious soul.

Chapter 17

Accepting change

In the 1970's, Alvin Toffler wrote that exceptionally rapid change is the hallmark of our era, coining the term 'future shock'. He argued that a new force, the 'accelerative thrust' had entered history and that individuals, organizations, society and the entire world were completely unprepared for dealing with it. International flight is a classic example, with jet-lag being the symptom of the body/brain needing extra time to catch up to the new time zone.

Since Toffler's thesis, information overload has become the norm. As we hurtle our way into the twenty-first century, five year-olds process hundreds of times more information in a single year than an adult existing at the beginning of the previous century did in their whole lifetime. Toffler argued that this phenomenon would overwhelm people, the accelerated rate of technological and social change leaving them disconnected and suffering from "shattering stress and disorientation". The theory was advanced that the prime objective of education should be to "increase the individual's 'cope-ability' - the speed and economy with which he can adapt to continual change."

Resistance to change, as we have already seen, is largely prompted by fear. Most people will cling to what is, even if it is not ideal, for fear of what may be worse. It's the old 'devil-you-know' syndrome. Why take the risk in the hope of finding something better? There may be nothing better out there – then the security of what was is lost. Best to stay in the existing comfort zone. It is a valid survival strategy but it is a limiting one. Change is a fact of life and there is no avoiding it. We can try to slow it down, but we cannot avoid it. There is nothing we now have or know, that will not change. Everything is in a state of becoming something else.

The more adaptable we can be the better. It is a fact that the more adaptable element in any situation is the one that controls the situation. Just as the supple tree bends to withstand the storm, so the less rigid mind maneuvers more deftly through the path of least resistance. Coming to a metaphorical road-block is an opportunity to find a new way. If the mind is cluttered with preconceived ideas, it is less able to shift direction. The still mind is an open mind. It is Zen mind, unencumbered by the past, open to dance lightly with grace and agility. This is the way to improve adaptability.

Priorities of concern

Rapid change is only one of the many challenges we face in life. Meaninglessness, lack of purpose, and spiritual hunger are just some of the others that might be included in a broader view. These are the things that are addressed when operating a small business and are the main reasons why it needs to be supported by the Zen Factor. It helps us to remember that what has meaning for us and what is meaningless, is something that we decide. There is a hierarchy in which we assign meaning, according to our priority at the moment. This is quite fluid and can change in an instant.

An example of this occurred to me when I was about six years old. Without a mother at home to take care of us during school holidays, our father sent us off to what was known as a 'health camp'. We slept in vast grey dormitories, high-ceilinged and cold. We ate at long trestle tables, the food cooked in huge vats like in soup-kitchens for the homeless. I usually finished everything on my plate, as our father had trained us to do. That night in the dorm, a few of the girls set up a wailing complaint about the food, moaning about how terrible it was, how it gave them belly-aches. I pulled the covers over my head, but still heard them carrying on.

'Was the food really that bad?' I wondered.

Perhaps it was. I had eaten it quite happily and felt fine. But then it occurred to me that this might be a game I could join in. I uncovered my face and let out a long, pained groan. Then another, even louder. Before long, I was making more noise than all the rest of them put together. And they stopped. They lost interest in their own belly-aching and came to my bedside, to offer comfort and consolation. The group consensus was that the food was bad, but that was now secondary to the plight of the youngest child. The priority had changed and a more compassionate view prevailed. It shows how quickly we can change our minds, especially when we relinquish identification.

Taking on giants

I have already made some mention of the trouble we cause for ourselves through attachment and identification. It is extremely valuable not only to recognize when this is happening, but also to have ways of breaking free of such limiting beliefs. While we might understand intellectually that our careers, social status, incomes or possessions are not I, it is less obvious to know the same about our body, thoughts, and feelings. It is necessary to develop a deeper, experiential awareness of this truth to be set free. All of our conditioning blinds us to this awareness and the group consensus informs us of its perceived 'reality'. We go around, clad in this marvelously complex machine, with scarcely ever a doubt that it is synonymous with the being that is perceived of as I myself. If everyone believes it to be so, it must be so. To stand apart from this, to question its validity, is like David taking on Goliath.

Having totally identified ourselves with the physical, mental or emotional aspects of our experience we remain lost to our true nature. A tool for unlocking this prison is described by G.I. Gurdjieff. I call it the Freedom from Identification meditation. It is one that is sure to alter the way we see ourselves and our world and provides the basis of fully appreciating our interconnectedness.

After entering a deeply meditative state of raised consciousness, contemplate the profound meaning behind each of these three statements:

"This is my body, it is not I."

"These are my thoughts, they are not I."

"These are my feelings, they are not I."

Consider each of these statements in turn, giving each one the patience, focus and attention needed to yield a deep understanding that begins with the intellect but moves beyond it to become a self-sustaining knowledge. By allowing the truth of each of these statements to be fully realized through direct experience you will come closer to an understanding of your true identity.

Many of us can understand on an intellectual level that we have a body, but we are not that body. It is more like the temporary shell of the hermit crab. We have a sense of an insubstantial existence apart from the mechanical form that houses us, perceiving instead what has been referred to as the 'ghost in the machine'. We have an understanding of a self that persists continuously throughout our lives, despite the enormous changes our physical bodies undergo from birth to death. Somehow we know that I am essentially the same person I have always been for as long as I can remember, even though my outer form is completely different from how it was when I was two and from how it will be when I am eighty or ninety. Certain aspects of my personality may have changed along the way, but there is a prevailing sense of continuity of identity aside from that. We might say things like "I used to be selfish but now I am more generous." Who is the I we are referring to here? Certainly not "selfish" or "generous", for these are personality traits that I can drop or acquire.

If the body was our true identity then it could wield autocratic power over us, but there have been many instances where this power has been over-ridden. Through meditation regimes or the prayer of healing ministries, people have been able to overcome terminal illnesses. The power of mind over matter is demonstrated in the 'placebo effect', which sees sugar pills to be almost as effective as the chemical medicine they stand for. Gurdjieff wrote of many seeming miracles that he witnessed in his travels throughout the Middle East, such as the instantaneous healing of an open wound in response to the toning of a particular vibration. We understand this now as sound therapy and recognize it as one small aspect of a rapidly developing field of vibrational medicine.

They are not I

So too, we have thoughts, but we are not our thoughts; we have feelings, but we are not our feelings. What then am 'I', if not my body, thoughts or feelings? The 'I' has been called the 'witness', something like a background observer, a consciousness that is able to remain detached from the puppet-show. Even this dispassionate witness is not our reality, for if something can be aware of itself, it cannot be the same as the object of its awareness. The best we can say is "I Am". Eckhart Tolle in *"A New Earth"* takes this as "incontrovertible evidence" for the immortality of our spirit, asking "How can I lose something that I Am?" at the time of our physical passing, and concluding, "It is impossible." This is not simply a play on words or vapid semantics but based on an experiential understanding of the nature of our essential being. The value of this understanding is in helping us to see others as ourselves and treat them accordingly.

Truth is obscured by our normal view of the world. Gurdjieff has suggested that if we were to take an about-face, a full one hundred and eighty degree turn, we might begin to come closer to reality. As it is, all that we hold near and dear serve as immovable blocks to our awareness of the truth. Similarly, intellectual theories about the nature of reality also create mental blocks, since truth can only be known directly. To quote from "*A Course In Miracles*":

"I do not know the thing I am, therefore do not know what I am doing, where I am, or how to look upon the world or myself. In this learning is salvation born. And what you are will tell you of Itself."

E-motion

One of the persistent themes of this book is that if we are able to change our thoughts we can change our world. All the sad, sorry, distressing thoughts of fear and attack, we can choose to let go of in exchange for happy thoughts of peace. It is up to us. When we find ourselves under the command of our emotions, it is useful to consider them as 'e-motion' or energy in motion. A simple analogy is to think of this energy as being contained in a row of bottles on a shelf. Each bottle has a label, such as 'anger', 'jealousy', 'fear', 'joy', 'love', etc. The energy inside each bottle is the same; only the labels differentiate them. We experience the force of the emotion not just as raw, undirected energy, but according to the label on the bottle.

It may seem that each label has been contextually applied or determined by external events. So we might tell ourselves, "this is a situation in which I should be jealous", or "this fact makes me feel sad". We have already seen that facts in themselves are completely neutral and have no power over how we feel. The way we interpret events is up to us and doesn't need to be dictated by convention or circumstance. We can recognize that every label has been chosen by us and is therefore under our control to remove. What remains, once we strip away the attribution of any particular label, is simply pure, undifferentiated energy.

How can we do this? Several of the Zen Factor tools already mentioned could be applied, as each aims to correct misconceptions about our true identity. In the spirit of Zen, it is a matter of letting things be as they are. We might regard the brain as a tangle of electrical impulses, trying to make sense of things by following the most comfortable ruts. When we regard it as a wayward wagon we can be more tolerant of its wanderings down dead-ends and attempt to guide it gently home.

The bottom line

All of these realizations will be of great benefit to us in our corporate roles. The more freedom we have, the more choices we have. The more we can recognize that our choices are our own, the more responsibility we take for them. Understanding that we are not our body, our thoughts or our feelings reminds us that in essence we are all the same. This increases our compassion and enables us to overlook what once we might have thought needed forgiveness. We are less likely to shoot from the hip when others slip up. We are less likely to have a grasping attitude or strive for personal gain at the expense of another. Identification with our achievements or possessions falls away. Acceptance of what is informs our being and is perfectly harmonized with the expansion of ourselves through living on purpose. The actualization of our dreams serves as an all-inclusive inspiration.

There is an old Irish joke about two brothers who buy a truckload of watermelons for a dollar each. They drive out and set up their stall at the side of the road where sell them all for a dollar each. At the end of the day, finding they have made no profit, Paddy scratches his head and says to his brother, "what we need is a bigger truck!"

In any kind of business, it is important to have the goal-posts set in advance and to keep a close watch on them to know when they have been reached. There are things known as KPI's (Key Performance Indicators) which will provide that information. Perhaps the most basic of these are gross and net profit. Gross profit is the difference between the cost of buying the watermelons and the price you sell them for. (Naturally, the greater the difference, the higher the gross profit will be). The bottom-line or net profit is the one to watch most closely. This is what is left after the costs of production, plus all other overheads such as salaries, rent, advertising and marketing costs, delivery truck, etc. have been removed. It is the net profit, or what's left in your pocket at the end of the day/year that matters.

In business, when products enter the global market-place, the sky really is the limit. The growth of the business becomes exponential rather than linear and everything speeds up. This was the stage things were at for me, when well over a million dollars worth of sales translated to a respectable net profit, given that overheads were relatively low and profit margins high. The loans had all been repaid and everything was now free and clear. My superannuation nest-egg held enough for a modest retirement. This was a great position to be in; one that I would have scoffed at had anyone suggested it in my earlier years.

The interesting thing is that using the tools of the Zen Factor to create this possibility had made it all seem perfectly natural and achievable. The high figures I was now dealing with had become simply numbers, with little emotional connection. A quarterly tax bill higher than most people's annual income did not even cause a flinch. I saw it as a positive reflection of how well things were going and looked forward to even higher bills. The higher the better! Rather than considering taxes an imposition, they can be seen as a marker of success; and for me, a way of paying back a debt to society that I had accrued as a single parent and student. For once I was on the giving, rather than receiving side. It felt an honor to be able to pay staff the salaries that enabled them to live comfortably and to contribute superannuation for their future retirement. There is a great sense of satisfaction comes from this kind of contribution, even if it is on a relatively small scale.

Letting go

Still, I could see that the time for me to hand over the reins was getting closer. It was obvious that there were others better placed to grow the business to its full potential. These firms had existing networks for distribution in place, far greater marketing budgets and the resources to develop a more extensive range of new products. And the fact was, it was never part of my long-term objectives to see that ultimate development through to its end. I had drawn the line in the sand right from the start and had no trouble letting go.

When it came time to step aside, I applied the tools of the Zen Factor to this outcome and was not disappointed. Quite incredibly everything was settled within two weeks of beginning negotiations with the potential buyers. This was a remarkable departure from the timeframe normally required for the sale of a business. Those handling the due diligence, paperwork and legal contracts did not believe it could be done so quickly. But in the same way that the rapid development of the business defied the common expectation, so too did its handover. In many ways it bore similarities to the sense of honor and gratitude that surrounded the passing and receiving of my beautiful yacht. This too was like handing over the Holy Chalice. I knew it was right.

As I stood sweeping the concrete floor of the empty warehouse it all seemed rather like a dream from which I was just awakening. So many massive changes had occurred in so short a time. This is precisely the prescription for future shock that Toffler wrote of, yet

I felt inwardly calm and at peace with myself. It had certainly been a roller-coaster ride and brought me to a place of new possibilities for the future. I had achieved my goals. I had the big boat and now had the time to sail it. I had bought the rest of my life, albeit in a humble way. Without the equanimity provided by the Zen Factor I am sure I would have suffered "shattering stress" and often felt overwhelmed or completely lost.

It is only by turning within, taking the time to get in touch with the quietude and certainty of purpose that exists like a lodestone in the central core of our being that we can avoid this disorientation. In quietude we can experience our purpose and our true nature. We can come to see that there exists a powerful force that is both within us and without, that is at once everywhere and nowhere. We cannot measure it, but we can certainly feel its presence, as real as love. It is this universal energy that gives us life and strength. Every one of us can tap into it if we choose to and allow its guiding light to reveal the manifestation of our wildest dreams.

About the author

Jacqueline Hope is a retired entrepreneur. She was first introduced to meditation in her early twenties through the work of G.I. Gurdjieff and later went on to explore other spiritual paths, including Sufism, Yoga, *"A Course In Miracles"* and Zen Buddhism. Through the use of these practices, she developed a highly successful small business, which, within a period of only three years, enabled her to achieve her goal of buying a big boat and sailing away. She now lives an endless summer cruising in the South Pacific and the Mediterranean.

www.ingramcontent.com/pod-product-compliance
Lightning Source LLC
Chambersburg PA
CBHW031236290426
44109CB00012B/323